VBScript
Pocket Reference

VBScript
Pocket Reference

Matt Childs,
Paul Lomax, and Ron Petrusha

O'REILLY®

Beijing • Cambridge • Farnham • Köln • Paris • Sebastopol • Taipei • Tokyo

VBScript Pocket Reference

by Matt Childs, Paul Lomax, and Ron Petrusha

Copyright © 2001 O'Reilly & Associates, Inc. All rights reserved. Printed in the United States of America.

Published by O'Reilly & Associates, Inc., 101 Morris Street, Sebastopol, CA 95472.

Editors: Ron Petrusha and Nancy Kotary

Production Editor: Jeffrey Holcomb

Cover Designer: Pam Spremulli

Printing History:

      January 2001:   First Edition

This book is based on information taken from O'Reilly's *VBScript in a Nutshell.*

CIP data can be found at *http://www.oreilly.com/catalog/vbscriptpr/*.

0-596-00126-6
[C]

Table of Contents

Alphabetical List of Entries

VBScript Pocket Reference

Introduction

Visual Basic Scripting Edition, or VBScript for short, is a member of the Visual Basic family of programming languages. Designed as a lightweight scripting language, it is a subset of Visual Basic for Applications (VBA), the programming language included as the centerpiece of Microsoft's retail Visual Basic product, as well as packaged as the programming language in a wide range of third party applications from Microsoft (e.g., the Microsoft Office suite) and third parties (e.g., AutoCAD, from AutoDesk).

VBScript is used primarily in the following four scripted environments:

- Active Server Pages (ASP), Microsoft's server-side scripting technology for Internet Information Server (IIS).

- Outlook forms. (Note that application level programming introduced in Outlook 2000 relies on VBA.)

- Windows Script Host (WSH), the scripting technology for automating the Windows desktop.

- Microsoft Internet Explorer (IE), where it is used for client-side scripting. Note, though, that non-Microsoft browsers either do not support client-side scripts or, like Netscape browsers, do not support VBScript as a scripting language.

VBScript Pocket Reference is a quick-reference guide to the VBScript language as of Version 5.5. It lists a concise description of all language elements by category for both

VBScript itself and for the Microsoft Scripting Runtime (*scrrun.dll*), an additional object library that provides support for associative arrays and filesystem access.

The purpose of this quick reference is to aid readers who need to look up some basic detail of VBScript syntax or usage. It is not intended to be a tutorial or user guide; at least a basic familiarity with VBScript is assumed. In addition, it does not explore the use of VBScript in any of the four scripted environments, nor does it document the objects and object models used in any of these four environments.

Font Conventions

`Constant Width`
> Used to indicate code examples, functions, statements, constants, constructs, and keywords.

`Constant Width Italic`
> Used to indicate user-defined variables that should be replaced with the appropriate text by the user.

Italic
> Used to indicate filenames, URLs, and email addresses.

Roman
> Used to indicate properties, procedures, methods, and objects, in addition to normal body text.

VBScript Conventions

The "rules" for writing scripts in VBScript are very simple:

- VBScript is a case-insensitive programming language; that is, case is ignored when reading VBScript scripts. So *myVar*, *MyVar*, *MYvar*, and *MYVAR* all refer to the same variable.

- Whitespace (except for line breaks) is ignored when reading VBScript scripts.

- Line breaks mark the end of a complete statement; complete VBScript statements must occupy a single line.

- If you want to break a single statement over several lines, you can use the line-continuation character, an underscore (_), which must be preceded by a space and must be the last character on the line that is to be continued.

- If you want to combine multiple statements on a single line, you can use the colon (:). For example, the multi-line code block:

```
If x < 100 Then
    x = x + 1
    y = y + 1
End If
```

can be shortened as follows:

```
If x < 100 Then x = x + 1: y = y + 1
```

- Two comment symbols are used: the apostrophe (') and the Rem keyword. They may appear at any place within a line. All code that follows the comment symbol is interepreted as a comment.

Datatypes

VBScript is a weakly typed language that has only a single datatype, the Variant, which can hold and in many cases seamlessly convert between data of different kinds. The particular kind of data held by a Variant at any given time is its *data subtype*. VBScript recognizes the following scalar data subtypes:

Empty
A declared but uninitialized variable

Byte
A signed 8-bit numeric datatype

Integer
A 16-bit numeric datatype

Long
A 32-bit numeric datatype

Single
A single-precision floating point value

Double
A double-precision floating point value

Currency
A currency value

Decimal
A decimal value

Date
A date or time value

Boolean
A logical (True or False) value

String
A variable-length character string

Object
A reference to an object

Nothing
An object variable not having a valid reference to an object

Null
Invalid data

In addition, VBScript supports both fixed and dynamic arrays. Each member of an array belongs to a particular scalar-data subtype or is another array. In other words, arrays can have a single dimension, or they can be multi-dimensional (up to 60 dimensions).

Variables

VBScript does not require that variables be declared before they are used unless you use the Option Explicit statement. In that case, you can declare variables using the Dim, Public, or Private statements.

A variable name in VBScript must satisfy the following requirements:

- It must be under 255 characters in length.
- It must begin with an alphabetic character.
- It cannot include embedded spaces.
- It cannot contain any special (i.e., nonalphabetic, non-numeric) character other than an underscore.
- It must be unique within its scope.

Operators and Precedence

Table 1 lists operators and a brief description.

Table 1. Operators and Their Functions

Operator	Description
+	Addition, string concatenation (not recommended)
-	Subtraction, unary operator
/	Division
\	Integer division (no remainder)
Mod	Modulo arithmetic
*	Multiplication
^	Exponentiation
&	String concatenation
=	Equality, assignment
Is	Equality (for object references)
<	Less than
<=, =<	Less than or equal to
>	Greater than
>=, =>	Greater than or equal to
<>, ><	Not equal to
And	Logical or bitwise conjunction
Or	Logical or bitwise disjunction
Not	Logical or bitwise negation
Eqv	Logical or bitwise equivalence

Table 1. Operators and Their Functions (continued)

Operator	Description
Imp	Logical or bitwise implication
Xor	Logical or bitwise exclusion

Expressions are evaluated in the following order:

1. Arithmetic operators
   a. Exponentiation
   b. Division and multiplication
   c. Integer division
   d. Modulo arithmetic
   e. Addition and subtraction
2. Concatenation operators
3. Logical operators
   a. Not
   b. And
   c. Or
   d. XOr
   e. Eqv
   f. Imp

If two or more operators in an expression have the same order of precedence, they are evaluated from left to right.

Constants

VBScript recognizes the following intrinsic constants:

- Color constants:
  vbBlack
  vbBlue
  vbRed

vbMagenta
vbGreen
vbCyan
vbYellow
vbWhite

- Comparison constants:

  vbBinaryCompare
  vbTextCompare

- Date and time constants:

  vbSunday
  vbMonday
  vbTuesday
  vbWednesday
  vbThursday
  vbFriday
  vbSaturday
  vbUseSystem
  vbUseSystemDayOfWeek
  vbFirstJan1
  vbFirstFourDays
  vbFirstFullWeek

- Date-format constants:

  vbGeneralDate
  vbLongDate
  vbLongTime
  vbShortDate
  vbShortTime

- Error constant:

  vbObjectError

- Logical and tristate constants:

  False
  True
  vbTrue
  vbFalse
  vbUseDefault

- Message-box constants/button constants:

  ```
  vbAbortRetryIgnore
  vbMsgBoxHelpButton
  vbOKCancel
  vbOKOnly
  vbRetryCancel
  vbYesNo
  vbYesNoCancel
  ```

- Default-button constants:

  ```
  vbDefaultButton1
  vbDefaultButton2
  vbDefaultButton3
  vbDefaultButton4
  ```

- Icon constants:

  ```
  vbCritical
  vbInformation
  vbExclamation
  vbQuestion
  ```

- Modality constants:

  ```
  vbApplicationModal
  vbSystemModal
  ```

- Return-value constants:

  ```
  vbAbort
  vbOK
  vbCancel
  vbRetry
  vbIgnore
  vbYes
  vbNo
  ```

- Miscellaneous constants:

  ```
  vbMsgBoxRight
  vbMsgBoxSetForeground
  vbMsgBoxRtlReading
  ```

- Special-character constants:

```
vbCr
vbNullChar
vbCrLf
vbNullString
vbFormFeed
vbTab
vbLf
vbVerticalTab
vbNewLine
```

- Variable-subtype constants:

```
vbArray
vbError
vbBoolean
vbInteger
vbByte
vbLong
vbCurrency
vbNull
vbDataObject
vbObject
vbDate
vbSingle
vbDecimal
vbString
vbDouble
vbVariant
vbEmpty
```

User-defined constants can be declared using the Const statement. In addition, using WSH and ASP, you may be able to access constants defined in type libraries as if they were intrinsic constants. In ASP, you use the METADATA tag in *global.asa*. For example, the following tag imports the constants defined in the Microsoft Scripting Runtime library:

```
<!--METADATA TYPE="TypeLib"
UUID="{420B2830-E718-11CF-893D-00A0C9054228}
-->
```

The UUID attribute requires the type library's interface identifier, which is defined in the HKEY_CLASSES_ROOT\TypeLib key of the system registry. You can also replace it with the FILE attribute and specify the path and filename of the type-library file:

```
<!--METADATA TYPE="TypeLib"
FILE="C:\windows\system32\scrrun.dll"
-->
```

In Windows Script Host, if you're using a Windows Script Host (*.wsf*) file, you can import a type library by including the XML <reference> tag, as follows:

```
<reference
GUID="{420B2830-E718-11CF-893D-00A0C9054228}"
/>
```

Functions and Subroutines

VBScript recognizes functions, which are declared with the Function...End Function construct, and subroutines, which are declared with the Sub...End Sub construct. Functions return a value to the caller; subroutines do not. Both functions and subroutines can include a list of parameters to be passed to the procedure by the caller. For example:

```
Public Function SwapNumbers(lNum1, lNum2)
    Dim lTemp
    lTemp = lNum2
    lNum2 = lNum1
    lNum1 = lTemp
    SwapNumbers = True
End Function
```

By default, arguments are passed to functions and subroutines *by reference*; that is, the address of the argument is provided to the function or subroutine, and any changes made to the argument by the function or subroutine are reflected when control returns to the caller. This behavior can be overridden, and an argument can be passed to a function or subroutine *by value*; that is, a copy of the data, rather than the address of the data, is provided to the function or subroutine, thus protecting variables from modification by a called procedure. To pass an argument by value, precede the parameter in the function or subroutine's parameter list with the ByVal keyword. You can also pass parameters explictly by reference by preceding the parameter name in the procedure declaration with the ByRef keyword.

You can call a subroutine in either of the following ways:

```
PrintIt oDoc
Call PrintIt(oDoc)
```

You call a function as follows (using our SwapNumbers function as an example):

```
bResult = SwapNumbers(lVar1, lVar2)
```

However, if you're not interested in the function's return value, you can also call the function as if it were a subroutine.

Program Structure

Structurally, any VBScript script consists of two possible parts:

Script-level
    Code that lies outside of functions and subroutines. In IE, Outlook forms, and WSH, script-level code is executed in a linear fashion. In ASP, the order of execution of script-level code in a <SCRIPT>...</SCRIPT> block is unpredictable, making the script level useful primarily for variable declaration. However, script-level code delimited by the <%...%> and <%=...%> tags is evaluated in the order in which it appears in the HTML stream.

Procedure-level
    Code found inside of procedures and functions.

The level at which a variable is declared determines its scope and lifetime. Script-level variables are visible throughout the script and its routines, and persist for the duration of the script. Procedure-level variables are local to the procedure in which they are declared and are destroyed when that procedure finishes executing.

Object-Oriented Programming

According to one definition, a scripting language is just "glue" used to hold together calls to various object methods and properties. For this purpose, VBScript provides the CreateObject function, which allows you to instantiate an object given its programmatic identifier, or ProgID. Once you can instantiate a creatable object in an object hierarchy, you can then use that object as the starting point to navigate an application's object model. The programmatic identifiers of some of the major object models that you might use in a VBScript script are:

ADODB.Connection
   The ADO Connection object

ADODB.Recordset
   The ADO Recordset object

Excel.Application
   The Microsoft Excel Application object

MAPI.Session
   A MAPI data store using Collaborative Data Objects (CDO)

Outlook.Application
   The Microsoft Outlook Application object

Scripting.Dictionary
   The Dictionary object of the Scripting Runtime

Scripting.FileSystemObject
   The FileSystemObject object of the Scripting Runtime

Word.Application
   The Microsoft Word Application object

In addition, development tools such as Visual Basic or Windows Script Components allow you to create custom components that can be instantiated using the CreateObject function.

Additional Information

You can get more information on VBScript, including documentation and the latest version of the software itself, from *http://msdn.microsoft.com/scripting/vbscript/*. Information on language elements and the versions of VBScript in which they are available can be found at *http://msdn.microsoft.com/scripting/vbscript/doc/vtoriversioninformation.htm*.

VBScript Reference

Array Handling

Array Function

```
Array([element1], [elementN],...)
```

element1
  Type: Required, Any

  The data to be assigned to the first array element.

elementN
  Type: Optional, Any

  Any number of data items you wish to add to the array.

Return Value

A Variant array consisting of the arguments passed into the function.

Description

Returns a Variant array containing the elements whose values are passed to the function as arguments.

The code fragment:

```
Dim vaMyArray
vaMyArray = Array("Mr", "Mrs", "Miss", "Ms")
```

is equivalent to writing:

```
Dim vaMyArray(3)
vaMyArray(0) = "Mr"
vaMyArray(1) = "Mrs"
vaMyArray(2) = "Miss"
vaMyArray(3) = "Ms"
```

Because `Array` creates a Variant array, you can pass any datatype, including objects, to the `Array` function. You can also pass the values returned by calls to other `Array` functions to create multidimensional arrays.

Dim Statement

```
Dim varname[([subscripts])],
varname[([subscripts])]
```

varname
   Type: Required

   Your chosen name for the variable.

subscripts
   Type: Optional

   Dimensions of an array variable.

Description

Declares and allocates storage space in memory for variables. When used in a procedure, the variable declared using `Dim` is local to that procedure. When used in a module or scripting block, it's available throughout the module. It is recommended, but not required, that `Dim` statements be placed at the beginning of the code block or procedure.

Erase Statement

```
Erase arraylist
```

arraylist
   Type: Required, Variant array

   A list of array variables to clear.

Description

Resets the elements of an array to their initial (unassigned) values. In short, `Erase` "clears out" or empties an array.

Filter Function

```
Filter(SourceArray, FilterString[,
      Switch[, Compare]])
```

SourceArray
> Type: Required, String or numeric

> An array containing values to be filtered.

FilterString
> Type: Required, String or numeric

> The string of characters to find in the source array.

Switch
> Type: Optional, Boolean

> A Boolean (True or False) value. If True (the default value), Filter includes all matching values in *result*; if False, Filter excludes all matching values (or, to put it another way, includes all nonmatching values).

Compare
> Type: Optional, Long

> An optional constant (possible values are 0, vbBinaryCompare; 1, vbTextCompare) that indicates the type of string comparison to use. The default value is 0, vbBinaryCompare

Return Value

A String array of the elements filtered from *SourceArray*.

Description

Produces an array of matching values from an array of source values that either match or don't match a given filter string. In other words, individual elements are copied from a source array to a target array if they either match or don't match a filter string.

IsArray Function

IsArray(*varname*)

varname
> Type: Required, Any

> The name of the variable to be checked.

Return Value

Boolean (True or False).

Description

Tests whether a variable is an array.

Join Function

```
result = Join(sourcearray, [delimiter])
```

sourcearray
    Type: Required, Variant

    Array whose elements are to be concatenated.

delimiter
    Type: Optional, String

    Character used to delimit the individual values in the string.

Return Value

A Variant of subtype String.

Description

Concatenates a single-dimensional array of values into a delimited string using a specified delimiter.

LBound Function

```
LBound(arrayname[, dimension])
```

arrayname
    Type: Required, Any

    The name of the array.

dimension
    Type: Optional, Long

    A number specifying the dimension of the array.

Return Value

A Variant of subtype Long.

Description

Determines the lower limit of a specified dimension of an array. All VBScript arrays are zero-based, meaning that the LBound function will always return 0.

ReDim Statement

```
ReDim [Preserve] varname(subscripts)
            [, varname(subscripts)] ...
```

Preserve

Type: Optional, Keyword

Preserves the data within an array when changing its single or last dimension. (If an array is contracted, data in the last elements will still be lost.)

varname

Type: Required, Any

Name of the variable.

subscripts

Type: Required

Number of elements and dimensions of the array, using the following syntax:

upper [, upper] ...

where *upper* is the upper bound of a particular array dimension.

Description

Resizes and reallocates storage space for a dynamic array.

Split Function

Split(*expression*,
    [*delimiter*[, *count*[, *compare*]]])

expression

Type: Required, String

A string to be broken up into multiple strings.

delimiter

Type: Optional, String

The character used to delimit the substrings in *expression*. If omitted, its value defaults to a blank space (" ").

count

Type: Optional, Long

The number of strings to return.

compare

Type: Optional, Long

The method of comparison. Possible values are the intrinsic VBScript constants vbBinaryCompare (0) or vbTextCompare (1).

Return Value

A Variant array.

Description

Parses a single string containing delimited values into an array.

Assignment

Set Statement

See "Set Statement" entry under "Object Programming."

Comment

' Statement; Rem Statement

```
Rem comment
' comment
```

comment
> Type: Optional
>
> A textual comment to place within the code.

Description

Use the Rem statement or an apostrophe (') to place remarks within the code.

Constants

Const Statement

```
[Public|Private] Const constantname = constantvalue
```

constantname
> Type: Required
>
> The name of the constant.

constantvalue
> Type: Required, Numeric or String
>
> A constant value and, optionally, arithmetic operators. Unlike variables, constants must be initialized.

Description

Declares a constant whose value can't be changed throughout the life of the program or routine. One of the ideas of declaring constants is to make code easier both to write and to read; it allows you to replace a value with a recognizable word.

Data Subtype Conversion

Asc, AscB, AscW Functions

Asc(*string*)
AscB(*string*)
AscW(*string*)

string
> Type: Required, String

> Any expression that evaluates to a string.

Return Value

An integer that represents the character code of the first character of the string. The range for the returned value is 0–255 on non-DBCS systems, but –32768–32767 on DBCS systems.

Description

Returns the ANSI (in the case of Asc) or Unicode (in the case of AscW) character code that represents the first character of the string passed to it. All other characters in the string are ignored. Use AscB with Byte data and AscW on Unicode (DBCS) systems.

CBool Function

CBool(*expression*)

expression
> Type: Required, String or Numeric

> Any numeric expression or a string representation of a numeric value.

Return Value

A Variant with a subtype of Boolean (True or False).

Description

Casts *expression* as a Variant with a Boolean subtype. Expressions that evaluate to 0 are converted to False (0), and expressions that evaluate to nonzero values are converted to True (–1).

CByte Function

CByte(*expression*)

expression
   Type: Required, Numeric or String

   A string or numeric expression that evaluates between 0 and 255.

Return Value

A Variant with a subtype of Byte.

Description

Converts *expression* to a Variant with a subtype of Byte. The byte is the smallest data subtype in VBScript. Being only one byte in length, it can store unsigned numbers between 0 and 255.

CCur Function

CCur(*expression*)

expression
   Type: Required, Numeric or String

   A string or numeric expression that evaluates to a number between −922,337,203,685,477.5808 and 922,337,203,685,477.5807.

Return Value

A Variant with a subtype of Currency.

Description

Converts *expression* into a Variant with a subtype of Currency.

CDate Function

CDate(*expression*)

expression
   Type: Required, String or Numeric
   Any valid date expression.

Return Value

A Variant with a Date subtype.

Description

Converts *expression* into a Variant of subtype Date.

CDbl Function

CDbl(*expression*)

expression
    Type: Required, Numeric or String

    Approximately −1.79769E308 to −4.9406564E−324 for negative values, and approximately 4.9406564E−324 to 1.797693E308 for positive values.

Return Value

A Variant with a Double subtype.

Description

Converts *expression* to a Variant with a Double subtype.

Chr, ChrB, ChrW Functions

Chr(*charactercode*)
ChrB(*charactercode*)
ChrW(*charactercode*)

charactercode
    Type: Required, Long

    An expression that evaluates to either an ASCII or DBCS character code.

Return Value

Variant of the subtype String that contains the character represented by *charactercode*.

Description

Returns the character represented by *charactercode*.

CInt Function

CInt(*expression*)

expression
    Type: Required, Numeric or String

    The range of *expression* is −32,768 to 32,767; fractions are rounded.

Return Value

A Variant of subtype Integer.

Description

Converts *expression* to a Variant with a subtype of Integer; any fractional portion of *expression* is rounded.

CLng Function

CLng(*expression*)

expression
> Type: Required, Numeric or String
>
> The range of *expression* is −2,147,483,648 to 2,147,483,647; fractions are rounded.

Return Value

A Variant with a subtype of Long.

Description

Converts *expression* to a Variant with a subtype of Long; any fractional element of *expression* is rounded.

CSng Function

CSng(*expression*)

expression
> Type: Required, Numeric or String
>
> The range of *expression* is −3.402823E38 to −1.401298E-45 for negative values; 1.401298E-45 to 3.402823E38 for positive values.

Return Value

A Variant with a subtype of Single.

Description

Returns a single-precision number.

CStr Function

CStr(*expression*)

expression
> Type: Required, Any
>
> Any expression that evaluates to a string.

Return Value

A Variant with a String subtype.

Description

Returns a string representation of *expression*.

DateSerial Function

See "DateSerial Function" entry under "Date and Time."

DateValue Function

See "DateValue Function" entry under "Date and Time."

Hex Function

Hex(*number*)

number
> Type: Required, Numeric or String
> A valid numeric or string expression.

Return Value

String representing the hexadecimal value of *number*.

Description

Returns a string that represents the hexadecimal value of a number.

Oct Function

Oct(*number*)

number
> Type: Required, Numeric or String
> Number or string representation of a number to convert.

Return Value

A Variant of subtype String.

Description

Returns the octal value of a given number.

TimeSerial Function

See "TimeSerial Function" entry under "Date and Time."

TimeValue Function

See "TimeValue Function" entry under "Date and Time."

Date and Time

Date Function

Date

Return Value

A Variant of subtype Date.

Description

Returns the current system date.

DateAdd Function

DateAdd(*interval, number, date*)

interval
    Type: Required, String

    An expression denoting the interval of time you need to add or subtract (see Table 2).

Table 2. Interval Settings

Setting	Description
yyyy	Year
q	Quarter
m	Month
y	Day of year
d	Day
w	Weekday
ww	Week
h	Hour
n	Minute
s	Second

number

Type: Required, Numeric expression

An expression denoting the number of time intervals you want to add or subtract. To subtract, *number* should be a negative value.

date

Type: Required, Date

A Variant of subtype Date or a literal denoting the date on which to base the DateAdd calculation.

Return Value

A Variant of subtype Date.

Description

Returns a date representing the result of adding or subtracting a given number of time periods to or from a given date or time. For instance, you can calculate the date 178 months before today's date, or the date and time 12,789 minutes from now. The calculated date, however, must not precede the year 100, or an error occurs.

DateDiff Function

```
DateDiff(interval, date1, date2
        [, firstdayofweek[, firstweekofyear]])
```

interval

Type: Required, String

The units of time used to express the result of the difference between *date1* and *date2* (see Table 3).

Table 3. Interval Settings

Setting	Description
yyyy	Year
q	Quarter
m	Month
y	Day of year
d	Day
w	Weekday

Table 3. Interval Settings (continued)

Setting	Description
ww	Week
h	Hour
n	Minute
s	Second

date1
> Type: Required, Date

> The first date you want to use in the differential calculation.

date2
> Type: Required, Date

> The second date you want to use in the differential calculation.

firstdayofweek
> Type: Optional, Numeric constant

> A numeric constant that defines the first day of the week. If not specified, Sunday is assumed (see Table 4).

Table 4. First Day of Week Constants

Constant	Value	Description
vbUseSystem	0	Use the NLS API setting
vbSunday	1	Sunday (default)
vbMonday	2	Monday
vbTuesday	3	Tuesday
vbWednesday	4	Wednesday
vbThursday	5	Thursday
vbFriday	6	Friday
vbSaturday	7	Saturday

firstweekofyear
> Type: Optional, Numeric constant

> A numeric constant that defines the first week of the year. If not specified, the first week is assumed to be the week in which January 1 occurs (see Table 5).

Table 5. First Week of Year Constants

Constant	Value	Description
vbUseSystem	0	Use the NLS API setting
vbFirstJan1	1	Start with the week in which January 1 occurs (default)
vbFirstFourDays	2	Start with the first week that has at least four days in the new year
vbFirstFullWeek	3	Start with first full week of the year

Return Value

A Variant of subtype Long specifying the number of time intervals between two dates.

Description

Calculates the number of time intervals between two dates. For example, can determine how many days there are between 1 January 1980 and 31 May 1998.

DatePart Function

```
DatePart(interval, date[,firstdayofweek
                    [, firstweekofyear]])
```

interval
    Type: Required, String

    The unit of time to extract from within *date* (see Table 6).

Table 6. Interval Settings

Setting	Description
yyyy	Year
q	Quarter
m	Month
y	Day of year
d	Day
w	Weekday
ww	Week
h	Hour
n	Minute
s	Second

date
> Type: Required, Date
>
> The Date value that you want to evaluate.

firstdayofweek
> Type: Optional, Numeric constant
>
> A numeric constant that defines the first day of the week. If not specified, Sunday is assumed (see Table 7).

Table 7. First Day of Week Constants

Constant	Value	Description
vbUseSystem	0	Use the NLS API setting
vbSunday	1	Sunday (default)
vbMonday	2	Monday
vbTuesday	3	Tuesday
vbWednesday	4	Wednesday
vbThursday	5	Thursday
vbFriday	6	Friday
vbSaturday	7	Saturday

firstweekofyear
> Type: Optional, Numeric constant
>
> A numeric constant that defines the first week of the year. If not specified, the first week is assumed to be the week in which January 1 occurs (see Table 8).

Table 8. First Week of Year Constants

Constant	Value	Description
vbUseSystem	0	Use the NLS API setting
vbFirstJan1	1	Start with week in which January 1 occurs (default)
vbFirstFourDays	2	Start with the first week that has at least four days in the new year
vbFirstFullWeek	3	Start with first full week of the year

Return Value

A Variant of subtype Integer.

Description

Extracts an individual component of the date or time (such as the month or the second) from a date/time value. `DatePart` is a single function encapsulating the individual `Year`, `Month`, `Day`, `Hour`, `Minute`, and `Second` functions.

DateSerial Function

`DateSerial(year, month, day)`

year
> Type: Required, Integer
>
> Number between 100 and 9999, inclusive, or a numeric expression.

month
> Type: Required, Integer
>
> Any numeric expression to express the month between 1 and 12.

day
> Type: Required, Integer
>
> Any numeric expression to express the day between 1 and 31.

Return Value

A Variant of subtype Date.

Description

Returns a date from the three date components (year, month, and day). For the function to succeed, all three components must be present, and all must be numeric values. The value returned by the function takes the short-date format defined by the Regional Settings applet in the Control Panel of the client machine.

DateValue Function

`DateValue(stringexpression)`

stringexpression
> Type: Required, String expression
>
> Any date expression recognized by `IsDate`.

Return Value

A Variant of subtype Date.

Description

Returns the date represented by *stringexpression*, formatted according to the short-date setting, which is defined by the Regional Settings applet in the Control Panel. DateValue doesn't return time values in a date/time string; they are simply dropped. However, if *stringexpression* includes a valid date value but an invalid time value, a runtime error results.

Day Function

Day(*dateexpression*)

dateexpression
    Type: Required, Any valid date expression

    Any expression capable of conversion to a Date.

Return Value

A Variant of subtype Integer.

Description

Returns a value ranging from 1 to 31, representing the day of the month of *dateexpression*. *dateexpression* must be a valid date/time or time value.

Hour Function

Hour(*time*)

time
    Type: Required, Any numeric or string expression

    Any valid date/time expression.

Return Value

A Variant of data subtype Integer.

Description

Extracts the hour element from a time expression.

Minute Function

Minute(*time*)

time
    Type: Required, Date/Time

    Any valid date/time expression, or an expression that can be evaluated as a date/time expression.

Return Value

A Variant of subtype Integer.

Description

Returns an integer between 0 and 59, representing the minute of the hour from a given date/time expression.

Month Function

Month(*date*)

date
> Type: Required, Any Variant capable of being expressed as a date
>
> Any valid date expression.

Return Value

A Variant integer between 1 and 12.

Description

Returns the month of the year of a given date expression.

MonthName Function

MonthName *monthnumber* [, *abbreviate*]

monthnumber
> Type: Required, Long
>
> The ordinal number of the month, from 1 to 12.

abbreviate
> Type: Optional, Boolean
>
> A flag to indicate whether an abbreviated month name should be returned.

Return Value

A Variant of subtype String.

Description

Returns the month name of a given month. For example, 1 returns January or, if *abbreviate* is True, Jan.

Now Function

Now( )

Return Value

A Variant of subtype Date.

Description

Returns the current date and time based on the system setting.

Second Function

Second(*time*)

time
> Type: Required, String, numeric, or Date/Time
>
> Any valid expression that can represent a time value.

Return Value

A Variant of subtype Integer in the range 0 to 59.

Description

Extracts the seconds from a given time expression.

Time Function

Time( )

Return Value

A Variant of subtype Date.

Description

Returns the current system time.

Timer Function

Timer( )

Return Value

A Variant of subtype Single.

Description

Returns the number of seconds since midnight.

TimeSerial Function

TimeSerial(*hour, minute, second*)

hour
>Type: Required, Integer
>
>A number in the range 0 to 23.

minute
>Type: Required, Integer
>
>Any valid integer.

second
>Type: Required, Integer
>
>Any valid integer.

Return Value

A Variant of subtype Date.

Description

Constructs a valid time given the number of hours, minutes, and seconds.

TimeValue Function

TimeValue(*time*)

time
>Type: Required, String
>
>Any valid string representation of a time.

Return Value

A Variant of subtype Date.

Description

Converts a string representation of a time to a Variant Date subtype.

Weekday Function

Weekday(*date*, [*firstdayofweek*])

date
>Type: Required, Variant
>
>Any valid date expression.

firstdayofweek
  Type: Optional, Integer

  Integer specifying the first day of the week.

Return Value

A Variant of subtype Integer.

Description

Determines the day of the week of a given date.

WeekdayName Function

```
WeekdayName(WeekdayNo, [abbreviate
          [, FirstDayOfWeek]])
```

WeekdayNo
  Type: Required, Long

  The ordinal number of the required weekday, from 1 to 7.
abbreviate
  Type: Optional, Boolean

  Specifies whether to return the full day name or an abbreviation.
FirstDayOfWeek
  Type: Optional, Integer

  Specifies which day of the week should be first.

Return Value

A Variant of subtype String.

Description

Returns the real name of the day.

Year Function

```
Year(date)
```

date
  Type: Required, Date

  Any valid date expression.

Return Value

A Variant of subtype Integer.

Description

Returns an integer representing the year in a given date expression.

Dictionary Object

Creatable

Yes

Description

The Dictionary object, which is found in the Microsoft Scripting Runtime (*scrrun.dll*), is similar to a Collection object, except that it is loosely based on the Perl associative array. Like an array or a Collection object, the Dictionary object holds elements, which are called *items* or *members*, containing data. Each member can be of any data subtype whatsoever, including objects and other Dictionary objects. You access the value of these dictionary items by using unique *keys* (or named values) that are stored along with the data, rather than by using the item's ordinal position, as you do with an array. This makes the Dictionary object ideal when you need to access data that is associated with a particular, unique named value. A very simple use of a Dictionary object is as a lookup table for state codes: each key corresponds to a state abbreviation, while the data value holds the full name of the state.

You can create a new instance of the Dictionary object by calling the CreateObject function with a ProgID of Scripting.Dictionary, as in the following code fragment:

```
Dim oDict
Set oDict = CreateObject("Scripting.Dictionary")
```

You can also use the object-creation facilities provided by your target runtime environment.

You can access each item stored to a Dictionary object by using the For Each...Next construct. However, rather than returning a Variant containing the stored data value to the Dictionary object as you would expect, it returns a Variant containing the key associated with the member. You then have to pass this key to the Item method to retrieve the member, as the following example shows:

```
Dim vKey
Dim sItem, sMsg
Dim oDict

Set oDict = CreateObject("Scripting.Dictionary")
oDict.Add "One", "Engine"
oDict.Add "Two", "Wheel"
oDict.Add "Three", "Tire"
oDict.Add "Four", "Spanner"
```

```
For Each vKey In oDict
   sItem = oDict.Item(vKey)
   sMsg = sMsg & sItem & vbCrLf
Next

MsgBox sMsg
Set oDict = Nothing
```

Dictionary Object Properties

The properties of the Dictionary object are read-write except for Count, which is read-only, and Key, which is write-only:

CompareMode (Long)
   Defines the type of text comparison in the Item property. Possible values are vbBinaryCompare (0) (the default) and vbTextCompare (1).

Count (Long)
   Indicates the total number of items in the dictionary.

Item (Any)
   Sets or retrieves a particular item of data in the dictionary. Its syntax is:

   ```
   oDict.Item(sKey)
   ```

   where *sKey* is the dictionary's key. When setting a key value, if *sKey* does not exist, a new member is added to the dictionary.

Key (String)
   Renames an existing key. Its syntax is:

   ```
   oDict.Key(sKey) = sName
   ```

   where *sKey* is the name of the key and *sName* is the new key name.

Dictionary Object Methods

The Dictionary object supports the following six methods:

Add
   Adds an item and its associated key to the dictionary. Its syntax is:

   ```
   oDict.Add sKey, vItem
   ```

   where *sKey* is a unique key name and *vItem* is the data value associated with the key.

Exists

Returns a Boolean indicating whether a particular key exists in the dictionary. Its syntax is:

```
oDict.Exists(sKey)
```

where *sKey* is the possible key name.

Items

Returns an array containing all data items in the dictionary. Its syntax is:

```
oDict.Items( )
```

Keys

Returns a Variant array containing all keys in the dictionary. Its syntax is:

```
oDict.Keys( )
```

Remove

Removes an item from the dictionary. Its syntax is:

```
oDict.Remove sKey
```

where *sKey* is the key associated with the data item to be removed.

RemoveAll

Removes all the data from the dictionary. Its syntax is:

```
oDict.RemoveAll( )
```

Error Handling

Err Object

Description

The Err object contains properties and methods that provide information about a single runtime error in a VBScript script. It also allows you to generate errors and reset the error object. Because the Err object is an intrinsic object with global scope, you don't need to create an instance of it within your code.

When an error is generated in your application—whether it's handled or not—the properties of the Err object are assigned values you can then access to gain information about the error that occurred. You can even generate your own errors explicitly using the Err.Raise method. You can also define your own errors to unify the error-handling process.

When your program reaches an `On Error Resume Next` statement, the Err object is cleared and its properties reinitialized. This can also be done explicitly using the Err.Clear method.

Properties

All Err object properties are read-write:

Description (String)
   The string describing the given error number

HelpContext (Long)
   The context ID of the relevant topic within a VBScript Help file

HelpFile (String)
   The path to a VBScript Help file

Number
   A long integer used to describe an error (i.e., an error code)

Source (String)
   Either the name of the current project or the class name of the application that generated the error

Methods

Clear
   Resets all the properties of the Err object. Its syntax is:

   `Err.Clear( )`

Raise
   Generates an error with a particular error code. Its syntax is:

   ```
   Err.Raise Number[, Source[, Description
                  [, HelpFile[, HelpContext]]]]
   ```

   where each parameter corresponds to the property of the same name.

On Error Statement

To enable error handling:

   `On Error Resume Next`

To disable error handling:

   `On Error Goto 0`

Description

Enables or disables error handling within a procedure. If you don't use an `On Error` statement in your procedure, or if you have explicitly switched off error handling, the VBScript runtime engine handles the error automatically. First, it displays a dialog containing the standard text of the error message, something many users are likely to find incomprehensible. Second, it terminates the application, so any error that occurs in the procedure produces a fatal runtime error.

File System Objects

Drive Object

Returned by

> File.Drive property
> FileSystemObject.Drives.Item property

Creatable

No

Library

Microsoft Scripting Runtime

Description

Represents a single drive connected to the current machine, including a network drive. By using the Drive object, you can interrogate the system properties of any drive. In addition, you can use the Folder object returned by the Drive object's RootFolder property as your foothold into the physical drive's filesystem.

A new instance of the Drive object cannot be created. Instead, a Drive object that represents an existing physical drive typically is retrieved from the FileSystemObject object's Drives collection, as in the following code fragment, which retrieves an object reference that represents the *C:* drive:

```
Dim oFS, oDrive
Set oFS = CreateObject("Scripting.FileSystemObject")
set oDrive = oFS.Drives("C")
```

Properties

All Drive object properties are read-only. In addition, removable media drives must be ready (i.e., have media inserted) for the Drive object to read certain properties:

AvailableSpace (Long)
> Returns the number of bytes unused on the disk. Typically, the AvailableSpace property returns the same number as the Drive

object's FreeSpace property, although differences may occur on systems that support quotas. In addition, because the property is a Variant Long, it is capable of storing only values that range from 0 to 2^{31}, or 2,147,483,648; in other words, in the case of large drives that have over 2 GB free, it fails to accurately report the amount of available free space.

In order to check the amount of available space on the drive, the drive must be ready or an error results. To prevent it, check the value of the IsReady property before attempting to retrieve a drive's free space.

DriveLetter (String)

The drive letter used for this drive on the current machine (e.g., *C*). In addition, its value is an empty string ("") if the drive is a network share that has not been mapped to a local drive letter.

DriveType (Long)

A value (see the following table) indicating the type of drive. Any remote drive is shown only as remote. For example, a shared CD-ROM or Zip drive that is both remote and removable is shown simply as remote (i.e., it returns a value of 3) on any machine other than the machine on which it's installed:

Constant	Value
CDROM	4
Fixed	2
RAM Disk	5
Remote	3
Removable	1
Unknown	0

The Scripting Runtime type library defines the constants shown in the previous table's Constant column. (Note that these are not intrinsic VBScript constants.) The DriveType property does not require that the drive be ready to return a value.

FileSystem (String)

The installed filesystem; returns FAT, FAT32, NTFS, or CDFS. In order to determine the filesystem in place, a device must be present on removable drives, or runtime error 71, "Disk not ready," results.

FreeSpace (Long)

The number of bytes unused on the disk. Typically, its value is the same as the Drive object's AvailableSpace property, although differences may occur on computer systems that support quotas.

Because the property is a Variant Long, it is capable of storing only values that range from 0 to 2^{31}, or 2,147,483,648. In other words, in the case of large drives that have over 2 GB free, it fails to accurately report the amount of available free space.

IsReady (Boolean)

For hard drives, should always return True. For removable media drives, True is returned if media is in the drive; otherwise, False is returned.

A number of Drive object properties raise an error if the drive they represent is not ready. You can use the IsReady property to check the status of the drive and prevent your script from raising an error.

Path (String)

The drive name followed by a colon (e.g., *C:*). (Note that it does not include the root folder.) This is the default property of the Drive object.

RootFolder (Folder object)

Gives you access to the rest of the drive's filesystem by exposing a Folder object representing the root folder.

SerialNumber (Long)

The serial number of the drive, which is an integer that uniquely identifies the drive or disk. If a disk or CD-ROM has been assigned a serial number, you can use this property to ensure that the correct disk is present in a drive that has removable media.

If a disk or CD-ROM has been assigned a serial number, you can use this property to ensure that the correct disk is present in a drive that has removable media.

ShareName (String)

For a network share, returns the machine name and share name in UNC format (e.g., *\\NTSERV1\TestWork*). If the Drive object does not represent a network drive, the ShareName property returns a zero-length string ("").

TotalSize (Long)

The total size of the drive in bytes. Because the TotalSize property is a Variant Long, it is capable of storing only values that range from 0 to 2^{31}, or 2,147,483,648. In other words, in the case of drives larger than 2 GB, it fails to accurately report the total drive size.

In order to check the amount of total space on the drive, the drive must be ready. Otherwise, a "Disk not ready" error is likely to result. This makes it worthwhile to check the value of the IsReady property before attempting to retrieve a drive's free space, particularly if your script is iterating the Drives collection.

VolumeName (String)

The drive's volume name, if one is assigned (e.g., *DRIVE_C*). If a drive or disk has not been assigned a volume name, the VolumeName property returns a null string (""). This is the only read/write property supported by the Drive object.

In order to retrieve the volume name, the drive must be ready. Otherwise, a "Disk not ready" error is likely to result. This makes it worthwhile to check the value of the IsReady property before attempting to retrieve a drive's volume name, particularly if your script is iterating the Drives collection.

Drives Collection Object

Returned by

FileSystemObject.Drives property

Creatable

No

Library

Microsoft Scripting Runtime

Description

All drives connected to the current machine are included in the Drives collection, even those that aren't currently ready (such as removable media drives with no media inserted in them). The Drives collection object is read-only.

The Drives collection cannot be created; instead, it is returned by the Drives property of the FileSystemObject object, as the following code fragment illustrates:

```
Dim oFS, oDrives
Set oFS = CreateObject("Scripting.FileSystemObject")
Set oDrives = oFS.Drives
```

Properties

Count (Long)

Returns the number of Drive objects in the collection.

Item (Drive object)

Syntax: oDrives.Item(*key*)

Returns a Drive object whose key is *key*, the drive letter. This is an unusual collection, since the drive's index value (its ordinal position in the collection) can't be used. Since attempting to retrieve a Drive object for a drive that doesn't exist generates runtime error 68, it's a good idea to call the FileSystemObject object's DriveExists method beforehand.

File Object

Creatable

No

Returned by

Files.Item property
FileSystemObject.GetFile method

Library

Microsoft Scripting Runtime

Description

The File object represents a disk file that can be a file of any type. The File object allows you to interrogate the properties of the file and to move upward in the filesystem hierarchy to interrogate the system on which the file resides. The process of instantiating a File object—for example, assigning a reference from the File object's Item property to a local object variable—doesn't open the file. An open file is represented in the File System object model by a Text-Stream object, which can be generated by the File object's OpenAsTextStream method.

There are several methods of retrieving a reference to an existing File object:

- If you want to work with a particular file, you can retrieve a reference to it directly by calling the GetFile method of the odFileSystemObject object. For example:

```
Dim oFS, oFile
Set oFS = CreateObject("Scripting.FileSystemObject")
Set oFile = oFS.GetFile("C:\Documents\MyReport.doc")
```

allows you to retrieve a reference to a File object representing the *MyReport.doc* file without having to use the File System object model to navigate the filesystem.

- If you want to work with a file as a member of a folder or of a set of files, you can retrieve a reference to a File object that represents the file from the Item property of the Files collection. (The Files collection is returned by the Files property of a Folder object.) The following code fragment, for instance, retrieves a reference to a file named *MyReport.doc* that is a member of the Documents folder:

```
Dim oFS, oFile
Set oFS = CreateObject("Scripting.FileSystemObject")
Set oFile = oFS.Drives("C").RootFolder. _
    SubFolders("Documents").Files("MyReport.doc")
```

Note that a File object represents an existing file; you cannot create a File object representing a new file. (You can, however, create a new TextStream object that represents a new text file by calling the Folder object's CreateTextFile method.)

Properties

Attributes (Long)
Sets or returns the file's attributes. The value of the property represents a bit mask consisting of six flags in the case of a File object, each of which represents a particular file attribute. These values are: 1, read-only; 2, hidden; 4, system; 32, archive, indicating that the file has not been backed up since it was created or last modified; 1024, alias; and 2048, compressed. All flags are read/write except for the alias and compressed flags. A value of 0 (normal) indicates that no flags are set.

DateCreated (Date)
The date and time the file was created; the property is read-only.

DateLastAccessed (Date)
The date and time the file was last accessed. Whether the property includes the date and time or only the date depends on the operating system; Win9x, for instance, only returns the date, while WinNT and Win2000 return the date and time. The property is read-only.

DateLastModified (Date)
The date and time the file was last modified; the property is read-only.

Drive (Drive object)

Returns a Drive object representing the drive on which the file resides; the property is read-only.

Name (String)

The name of the file. Modifying the value of a File object's Name property renames the file.

ParentFolder (Folder object)

Returns a Folder object representing the folder in which the file resides; the property is read-only.

Path (String)

Returns the full path to the file from the current machine, including drive letter or network path/share name; the property is read-only. Path is the default property of the File object.

ShortName (String)

Returns a DOS 8.3 filename; may not work on an NTFS system.

ShortPath (String)

Returns a DOS 8.3 folder name; may not work on an NTFS system. The property is read-only.

Size (Long)

Returns the size of the file in bytes. The property is read-only.

The Size property holds a long integer, meaning that it accurately reports file sizes from 0 to 2,147,483,648 bytes. In other words, in the case of large files over 2 GB in size, it fails to accurately report the size.

Type (String)

Returns a string containing the registered file-type description. This is the type string displayed for the file in Windows Explorer. If a file doesn't have an extension, the type is simply "File." When a file's type isn't registered, the type appears as the extension and "File." The property is read-only.

Methods

The File object supports the following four methods:

Copy

Copies the file to another location. Its syntax is:

```
oFile.Copy Dest [, Overwrite]
```

where *Dest* is the path and optionally the filename of the target file, and *Overwrite* is a Boolean indicating whether the file should be overwritten if it exists. By default, *Overwrite* is True.

Delete

Removes the file. Its syntax is:

```
oFile.Delete [Force]
```

where *Force* is a Boolean that determines whether the file should be deleted even if it is read-only. By default, *Force* is False.

Move

Moves the file from its current location. Its syntax is:

```
oFile.Move Dest
```

where *Dest* is the path to which the file should be moved.

OpenAsTextStream

Opens the file and returns a TextStream object representing the file's contents. Its syntax is:

```
oFile.OpenAsTextStream([IOMode[, Format]])
```

where *IOMode* indicates how the file is opened (choices are ForReading, 1, the default; ForWriting, 2; and ForAppending, 8), and *Format* indicates whether the file should be opened as an ASCII or Unicode file (choices are TristateFalse, 0; TristateTrue, −1; and TristateUseDefault, −2, the default).

Files Collection Object

Creatable

No

Returned by

Folder.Files property

Library

Microsoft Scripting Runtime

Description

The Files collection object is a container for File objects that is returned by the Files property of any Folder object. All files contained in the folder are included in the Files collection object. You can obtain a reference to a Files collection object using a code fragment like the following:

```
Dim oFS, oFiles

Set oFS = CreateObject("Scripting.FileSystemObject")
Set oFiles = oFS.Drives("C:").RootFolder. _
             SubFolders("Windows").Files
```

This code returns the Files collection for the Windows folder.

You can obtain a reference to an individual File object using the Files collection object's Item property; this takes the exact filename, including the file extension, as an argument. To iterate through the collection, you can use the For Each...Next statement.

Properties

The Files collection object is read-only. Consequently, it supports only the following two properties:

Count (Long)
Returns the number of File objects in the collection.

Item (File object)
Takes the filename (including the file extension) as a parameter and returns the File object representing the file with that name. Individual File objects can't be accessed by their ordinal position in the collection. Item is the Files collection object's default property. The following code fragment uses the Item property to retrieve the *autoexec.bat* File object:

```
Dim ofsFiles
Dim ofsFile

Set ofsFileSys = _
    CreateObject("Scripting.FileSystemObject")
Set ofsFiles = ofsFileSys.Drives("C").RootFolder.Files
Set ofsFile = ofsFiles.Item("autoexec.bat")
```

FileSystemObject Object

Creatable

Yes

Library

Microsoft Scripting Runtime

Description

The FileSystemObject object is at the top level of the File System object model and is the only externally creatable object in the hierarchy; that is, it's the only object you can create using the CreateObject function or the host object model's object-creation facilities. For example, the following code instantiates a FileSystemObject object named oFS:

```
Dim oFS
Set oFS = CreateObject("Scripting.FileSystemObject")
```

The FileSystemObject object represents the host computer's file-system as a whole. Its members allow you to begin navigation into the filesystem, as well as to access a variety of common filesystem services.

Properties

The FileSystemObject object has a single read-only property, Drives, which represents the pathway into the filesystem:

Drives (Drives Collection object)
Returns a Drives collection, each member of which is a Drive object representing a single drive available on the system.

Methods

Many FileSystemObject methods are parsing functions; they extract some portion of a path or filename without verifying the validity of either the parsed string or the result:

BuildPath
Returns a single string containing a path and filename or simply a complete path by concatenating its arguments and adding, where required, the correct path separator for the host system. Its syntax is:

```
oFS.BuildPath(sPath, sName)
```

where *sPath* is a path and *sName* is a path, a filename, or a path and filename.

CopyFile
Copies a file from one folder to another. Its syntax is:

```
oFS.CopyFile Source, Dest [, Overwrite]
```

where *Source* is the path and filename of the file to be copied, *Dest* is the path and optionally the filename of the target file, and *Overwrite* is a Boolean that indicates whether the target file should be overwritten if it already exists. The default value of *Overwrite* is True.

CopyFolder
Copies the contents of one or more folders, including subfolders, to another location. Its syntax is:

```
oFS.CopyFolder Source, Dest [, Overwrite]
```

where *Source* is the path and name of the source folder, *Dest* is the path of the target folder, and *Overwrite* is a Boolean that indicates whether existing files are to be overwritten. The default value of *Overwrite* is True.

CreateFolder

Creates a new folder and returns a new Folder object representing that folder. Its syntax is:

```
oFS.CreateFolder(Path)
```

where *Path* is the path and name of the folder to be created.

CreateTextFile

Creates a new file and returns its TextStream object. Its syntax is:

```
oFS.CreateTextFIle(Filename [, Overwrite
                            [, Unicode]])
```

where *Filename* is the path and name of the file to create, *Overwrite* is a Boolean that indicates whether the file should be overwritten if it already exists, and *Unicode* is a Boolean that indicates whether *Filename* is to be written as an ASCII or a Unicode file.

DeleteFile

Permanently deletes a file or set of files. Its syntax is:

```
oFS.DeleteFile FileSpec [, Force]
```

where *FileSpec* is a file specification that can include wildcard characters, and *Force* is a Boolean that determines whether read-only files can be deleted. Its default value is False.

DeleteFolder

Permanently removes one or more folders and their subfolders. Its syntax is:

```
oFS.DeleteFlder FileSpec [, Force]
```

where *FileSpec* is a file specification that can include wildcard characters, and *Force* is a Boolean that determines whether read-only folders can be deleted. Its default value is False.

DriveExists

Returns a Boolean indicating whether a specified drive exists on the local machine or the network. Its syntax is:

```
oFS.DriveExists(sDrive)
```

where *sDrive* is a string containing the drive name.

FileExists

Returns a Boolean indicating whether a specified file exists. Its syntax is:

```
oFS.FileExists(sFile)
```

where *sFile* is the path and name of the file.

FolderExists

Returns a Boolean indicating whether a specified folder exists. Its syntax is:

```
oFS.FolderExists(sFolder)
```

where *sFolder* is the path and name of the folder.

GetAbsolutePathName

Converts a relative path to a fully qualified path, including the drive letter, which is returned by the function. Its syntax is:

```
oFS.GetAbsolutePathName(Path)
```

where *Path* is a relative path.

GetBaseName

Returns the name of the last path component without an extension, if one is present. Its syntax is:

```
oFS.GetBaseName(Path)
```

where *Path* is a complete path specification.

GetDrive

Returns a Drive object representing a designated drive. Its syntax is:

```
oFS.GetDrive(Drive)
```

where *Drive* is a string containing the name of the drive.

GetDriveName

Extracts and returns the drive name from a path. Its syntax is:

```
oFS.GetDriveName(Path)
```

where *Path* is the path containing a drive name.

GetExtensionName

Returns the file extension in a path. Its syntax is:

```
oFS.GetExtensionName(Path)
```

where *Path* is a path specification.

GetFile

Returns a File object. Its syntax is:

```
oFS.GetFile(Path)
```

where *Path* is the path and name of the file.

GetFileName

Extracts and returns the filename from a complete path. Its syntax is:

```
oFS.GetFileName(Path)
```

where *Path* is a string containing the path and name of the file.

GetFolder
> Returns a Folder object. Its syntax is:
>
> ```
> oFS.GetFolder(Path)
> ```
>
> where *Path* is the path to the folder.

GetParentFolderName
> Returns the parent of a file or folder. Its syntax is:
>
> ```
> oFS.GetParentFolderName(Path)
> ```
>
> where *Path* is the complete path and filename of a file or folder whose parent is to be returned.

GetSpecialFolder
> Returns a reference to a Folder object representing the Windows folder, the Windows system folder, or the Windows Temporary folder. Its syntax is:
>
> ```
> oFS.GetSpecialFolder(FolderType)
> ```
>
> where *FolderType* can be SystemFolder (1), TemporaryFolder (2), or WindowsFolder (0).

GetStandardStream
> Returns a TextStream object representing standard input, standard output, or the standard error stream. Its syntax is:
>
> ```
> oFS.GetStandardStream(Type [, Unicode])
> ```
>
> where *Type* is the stream type (StdIn, 0; StdOut, 1; and StdErr, 2), and *Unicode* is a Boolean indicating whether the stream is Unicode or ASCII.

GetTempName
> Returns a system-generated temporary filename or folder name, but does not actually create the file or folder. Its syntax is:
>
> ```
> oFS.GetTempName()
> ```

MoveFile
> Moves one or more files from one folder to another. Its syntax is:
>
> ```
> oFS.MoveFile Source, Dest
> ```
>
> where *Source* is a path with optional wildcard characters that identifies one or more files, and *Dest* is the path of the folder to which the files will be moved.

MoveFolder
> Moves one or more folders, along with their files and subfolders, to a new location. Its syntax is:
>
> ```
> oFS.MoveFolder Source, Dest
> ```

---

where *Source* is a path with optional wildcard characters that identifies one or more folders, and *Dest* is the path of the folder to which the folders will be moved.

OpenTextFile

Optionally creates and opens a text file and returns its Text-Stream object. Its syntax is:

```
oFS.OpenTextFile(Filename [, IOMode[, Create
                 [, Format]]])
```

where *Filename* is the path and name of the file to open; *IOMode* indicates whether it should be opened ForAppending (0), ForReading (1, the default value), or ForWriting (2); *Create* is a Boolean that indicates whether the file should be created if it doesn't exist; and *Format* defines whether the file should be opened as a Unicode or ASCII file. Possible values for *Format* are TriStateUseDefault (-2), the default; TriStateTrue (-1) for Unicode; and TriStateFalse (0) for ASCII.

Folder Object

Creatable

No

Returned by

Drive.RootFolder property
FileSystemObject.CreateFolder method
FileSystemObject.GetFolder method
Folder.SubFolders.Item property
Folders.Add method

Library

Microsoft Scripting Runtime

Description

The Folder object allows you to interrogate the system properties of the folder and provides methods that allow you to copy, move, and delete the folder. You can also create a new text file within the folder.

The Folder object is unusual because with it, you can gain access to a Folders collection object. The more usual method is to extract a member of a collection to gain access to the individual object. However, because the Drive object exposes only a Folder object for the root folder, you have to extract a Folders collection object from a Folder object (the collection represents the subfolders of the root). From this collection, you can navigate downward through the

---

filesystem to extract other Folder objects and other Folders collections. A Boolean property, IsRootFolder, informs you of whether the Folder object you are dealing with is currently the root of the drive.

The Folder object is one of the objects in the File System object model; for an overview of the model, see the "FileSystemObject Object" entry.

Properties

Attributes (Long)
A set of flags representing the folder's attributes. The flags that apply to folders are:

Constant	Value
Archive	32
Directory	16
Hidden	2
ReadOnly	1
System	4

These attribute flags are represented by constants in the Scripting Runtime Library; they are not intrinsic VBScript constants.

You can determine which flag is set by using a logical And, along with the value returned by the property and the value of the flag you'd like to test. For example:

```
If oFolder.Attributes And ReadOnly Then
    ' Folder is read-only
```

To clear a flag, And the value of the Attributes property with a Long in which the flag you want to clear is turned off. For example, the following code clears a Folder object's read-only flag:

```
oFile.Attributes = oFileAttributes And (Not ReadOnly)
```

Date Created (Date)
The date and time the folder was created.

DateLastAccessed (Date)
The date and, if it's available from the operating system, the time that the folder was last accessed.

DateLastModified (Date)
The date and time the folder was last modified.

Drive (Drive object)
Returns a Drive object representing the drive on which this folder resides; the property is read-only.

Files (Files collection object)
Returns a read-only Files collection object representing all files in the current folder.

IsRootFolder (Boolean)
Returns True if the folder is the root folder of its drive.

Name (String)
Returns the name of the folder.

ParentFolder (Folder object)
Returns a Folder object representing the parent folder of the current folder. It returns Nothing if the current object is the root folder of its drive (i.e., if its IsRootFolder property is True).

Path (String)
Returns the complete path of the folder, including its drive. It is the default property of the Folder object.

ShortName (String)
Returns a DOS 8.3 folder name without the folder's path. May not work on an NTFS system. The property is read-only.

ShortPath (String)
Returns the complete path to a folder in DOS 8.3 format. May not work on an NTFS system. The property is read-only.

Size (Long)
Returns the complete size of all files, subfolders, and their contents in the folder structure, starting with the current folder. The property is read-only.

The Size property is a Variant Long, which can accurately report file sizes from 0 to 2,147,483,648 bytes. It fails to accurately report the size of a folder whose files and subfolders occupy more than 2 GB.

Attempting to retrieve the value of a Folder object's Size property when that folder is a drive's root folder (that is, its IsRootFolder property returns True) generates runtime error 76, "Path not found."

SubFolders (Folders collection object)
Returns a Folders collection object representing all subfolders within the current folder.

Type (String)
Returns the description of a File System object, as recorded in the system registry. For Folder objects, the property always returns "File Folder."

Methods

The Folder object supports the following four methods:

Copy

Copies the folder and its contents, including subfolders, to another location. Its syntax is:

```
oFolder.Copy Dest [, Overwrite]
```

where *Dest* is the destination path, and *Overwrite* is a Boolean indicating whether files and folders should be overwritten if they exist. By default, *Overwrite* is True.

CreateTextFile

Returns a write-only TextStream object representing a new file that is created in the folder. Its syntax is:

```
oFolder.CreateTextFile(Name[, Overwrite[,
                        Unicode]])
```

where *Name* is the complete filename, *Overwrite* is a Boolean indicating whether an existing file should be overwritten (its value defaults to False), and *Unicode* is a Boolean indicating whether a Unicode or an ASCII file is to be created. The default value of *Unicode* is False; an ASCII file will be created.

Delete

Permanently removes the folder, as well as any files and sub-folders. Its syntax is:

```
oFolder.Delete [Force]
```

where *Force* is a Boolean that determines whether the folder should be deleted even if it is read-only. By default, *Force* is False.

Move

Moves the folder, along with its files and subfolders, from its current location. Its syntax is:

```
oFolder.Move Dest
```

where *Dest* is the destination path of the folder.

Folders Collection Object

Creatable

No

Returned by

Folder.SubFolders property

Library

Microsoft Scripting Runtime

Description

The Folders collection object is a container for Folder objects. Normally, you'd expect to access a single object from the collection of that object; for example, you'd expect to access a Folder object from the Folders collection object. However, things are the other way around here: you access the Folders collection object from an instance of a Folder object. This is because the first Folder object you instantiate from the Drive object is a Root Folder object, and from it you instantiate a subfolders collection. You can then instantiate other Folder and subfolder objects to navigate through the drive's filesystem.

The Folders collection is a subfolder of any Folder object. For instance, the top-level Folders collection (representing all of the folders in the root directory of a particular drive) can be instantiated as follows:

```
Dim oFS, oFolders
Set oFS = _
WScript.CreateObject("Scripting.FileSystemObject")
Set oFolders = oFS.Drives("C").RootFolder.SubFolders
```

Properties

Item (Folder object)
> Retrieves a particular Folder object from the Folders collection object. You can access an individual folder object by providing the exact name of the folder without its path. However, you can't access the item using its ordinal number. For example, the following statement returns the Folder object that represents the *roottwo* folder:

```
Set ofsSubFolder = ofsSubFolders.Item("roottwo")
```

Count, Long
> The number of Folder objects contained in the Folders collection.

Methods

Add
> Returns a reference to a new folder that is added to the parent folder's Folders collection. Its syntax is:

```
oFolders.Add(Name)
```

where *Name* is the name of the new folder.

TextStream Object

Creatable

No

Returned by

    File.OpenTextStream method
    FileSystemObject.CreateTextFile method
    FileSystemObject.GetStandardStream method
    FileSystemObject.OpenTextFile method
    Folder.CreateTextFile method

Library

    Microsoft Scripting Runtime
    Windows Script Host

Description

Most commonly, the TextStream object represents a text file. As of Windows Script Host 2.0 and VBScript 5.5, however, it also represents any input/output stream, such as standard input, standard output, and the standard error stream. Depending on the precise character of the I/O stream, you can open a TextStream object to read from, append to, or write to the stream. The TextStream object provides methods to read, write, and close the text file or I/O stream.

When dealing with files, note that the TextStream object represents the file's contents or internals; the File object represents the file's externals or the file as an object in the filesystem.

Properties

The availability of TextStream object properties depends on the precise character of the TextStream object. Some properties are available only when the stream is opened in read mode (indicated by an R in the Availability field); others are available in both read and write modes (indicated by a RW in the Availability field). All of the following TextStream object properties are read-only:

AtEndOfLine (Boolean)
    Availability: R

    A flag denoting whether the end of a line marker has been reached (True) or not (False). Relevant only when reading a file.

    When reading a standard input stream from the keyboard, the end of a line is indicated by pressing the Enter key.

AtEndofStream (Boolean)
  Availability: R

  A flag denoting whether the end of the stream has been reached (True) or not (False). Relevant only when reading a file.

  When reading a standard input stream from the keyboard, the end of the input stream is indicated by the Ctrl-Z character.

Column (Long)
  Availability: RW

  Returns the column number position of the file marker. The first column position in the input stream and in each row is 1.

  Examining the value of the Column property is most useful in input streams after calls to the TextStream object's Read and Skip methods. Although it is less useful for output streams, it can be used after a call to the TextStream object's Write method.

Line (Long)
  Availability: RW

  Returns the line number position of the file marker. Lines in the text stream are numbered starting at 1.

  Unless the end of the text stream has been reached, the value of the Line property is incremented after calls to the ReadAll, ReadLine, and SkipLine methods. Similarly, in output streams it is incremented after calls to the WriteLine and WriteBlankLines methods.

Methods

The TextStream object supports the following nine methods:

Close
  Closes the open TextStream object. Its syntax is:

  ```
  oTS.Close( )
  ```

Read
  Reads a given number of characters from a readable Text-Stream object (a file or the standard input) and returns the resulting string. Its syntax is:

  ```
  oTS.Read(Characters)
  ```

  where *Characters* is the maximum number of characters to read from the input stream.

ReadAll
  Reads the entire contents of a readable TextStream object (a file or the standard input stream) and returns the resulting string. Its syntax is:

  ```
  oTS.ReadAll( )
  ```

ReadLine
> Reads an entire line from a readable TextStream object (a file or the standard input stream) and returns the resulting string except for the end-of-line character. Its syntax is:

```
oTS.ReadLine( )
```

Skip
> Ignores a given number of characters when reading from an input stream. Its syntax is:

```
oTS.Skip NChars
```

> where *NChars* is the number of characters to skip.

SkipLine
> Ignores the current line when reading from an input stream. Its syntax is:

```
oTS.SkipLine( )
```

Write
> Writes a string to an output stream (a text file, standard output, or standard error). Its syntax is:

```
oTS.Write Text
```

> where *Text* is the text to write to the output stream.

WriteBlankLines
> Inserts one or more newline characters into the output stream. Its syntax is:

```
oTS.WriteBlankLines(NLines)
```

> where *NLines* is the number of newline characters to write.

WriteLine
> Writes a string to the output stream and automatically appends a newline character. Its syntax is:

```
oTS.WriteLine Text
```

> where *Text* is the text to write to the output stream.

Information Functions

GetLocale Function

```
GetLocale( )
```

Return Value

A Variant of subtype Long

Description

Returns the locale ID, a 32-bit value that reflects a set of language, country, and cultural preferences. For example, the local ID of U.S. English is 1033.

IsArray Function

See "IsArray Function" entry under "Array Handling."

IsDate Function

IsDate(*expression*)

expression
> Type: Required, Any expression capable of conversion to a date or time.
>
> Variable or expression containing a date or time.

Return Value

Boolean (True or False).

Description

Determines whether a variable's value can be converted to a date.

IsEmpty Function

IsEmpty( )

varname
> Type: Required, Variant
>
> A numeric or string expression.

Return Value

Boolean (True or False).

Description

Determines if the variable has been initialized by having an initial value (other than Empty) assigned to it.

IsNull Function

IsNull(*expression*)

expression
> Type: Required, Any Variant
>
> An expression containing string or numeric data.

Return Value

Boolean (True or False).

Description

Determines whether *expression* contains any null data.

IsNumeric Function

IsNumeric(*expression*)

expression
  Type: Required, Any numeric or string expression
  A numeric or string expression.

Return Value

Boolean (True or False).

Description

Determines whether *expression* can be evaluated as a number.

IsObject Function

IsObject(*varname*)

varname
  Type: Required, Any
  Name of the variable to be evaluated

Return Value

Boolean (True or False).

Description

Indicates whether a variable contains a reference to an object—in other words, if it's an object variable.

Len, LenB Functions

Len(*string* | *varname*)

string
  Type: Required, String
  A valid string expression.

varname
>   Type: Required, Any except object

>   A valid variable name.

Return Value

A Variant of subtype Long.

Description

Counts the number of characters within a string or the size of a given variable. Use LenB to determine the actual number of bytes required to hold a given variable in memory.

RGB Function

RGB(*red, green, blue*)

red
>   Type: Required, Integer

>   A number between 0 and 255, inclusive.

green
>   Type: Required, Integer

>   A number between 0 and 255, inclusive.

blue
>   Type: Required, Integer

>   A number between 0 and 255, inclusive.

Return Value

A Long integer representing the RGB color value.

Description

Returns a system color code that can be assigned to object color properties.

ScriptEngine Function

ScriptEngine( )

Return Value

A Variant of subtype String.

Description

Indicates the scripting language currently in use.

ScriptEngineBuildVersion Function

```
ScriptEngineBuildVersion( )
```

Return Value

A Variant of subtype Long.

Description

Returns the build number of the VBScript scripting engine.

ScriptEngineMajorVersion Function

```
ScriptEngineMajorVersion( )
```

Return Value

A Variant of subtype Long.

Description

Indicates the major version (1, 2, and so on) of the scripting language currently in use.

ScriptEngineMinorVersion Function

```
ScriptEngineMinorVersion( )
```

Return Value

A Variant of subtype Long.

Description

Indicates the minor version (the number to the right of the decimal point) of the scripting language engine currently in use.

SetLocale Function

```
SetLocale(lcid)
```

lcid
   Type: Required, Long
   A valid geographical-locale ID.

Return Value

A Variant of subtype Long.

Description

Sets the system's geographical locale to *lcid* and returns the system's previous locale.

TypeName Function

TypeName(*varname*)

varname
    Type: Required, Any
    The name of a variable.

Return Value

A Variant of subtype String.

Description

Returns a string containing the name of the data subtype of a variable. An array is indicated by the string Variant.

VarType Function

VarType(*varname*)

varname
    Type: Required
    The name of a variable.

Return Value

A Variant of subtype Integer representing the data subtype of *varname*.

Description

Determines the data subtype of a specified variable.

Mathematical and Numeric

Abs Function

result = Abs(*number*)

number
    Type: Required, Any valid numeric expression
    The number whose absolute value is to be returned.

Return Value

The absolute value of *number*. The datatype is the same as that passed to the function.

Description

Returns the absolute value of a number (i.e., its unsigned magnitude). For example, Abs(-1) and Abs(1) both return 1. If *number* contains Null, Null is returned; if it's an uninitialized variable, zero is returned.

Atn Function

Atn(*number*)

number
> Type: Required, Numeric
>
> Any numeric expression, representing the ratio of two sides of a right-angle triangle.

Return Value

A Variant of subtype Double in the range –pi/2 to pi/2 radians.

Description

The arctangent function, it takes the ratio of two sides of a right triangle (*number*) and returns the corresponding angle in radians. The ratio is the length of the side opposite the angle divided by the length of the side adjacent to the angle.

Cos Function

Cos(*number*)

number
> Type: Required, Numeric expression
>
> An angle in radians.

Return Value

A Variant with a subtype of Double denoting the cosine of an angle.

Description

The cosine function takes an angle specified in radians and returns a ratio representing the length of the side adjacent to the angle divided by the length of the hypotenuse.

Exp Function

Exp(*number*)

number
> Type: Required, Number
>
> Any valid numeric expression.

Return Value

A Variant of subtype Double.

Description

Returns the antilogarithm of a number; the antilogarithm is the base of natural logarithms, e (whose value is the constant 2.7182818), raised to a power.

Fix Function

Fix(*number*)

number
> Type: Required, Numeric
>
> Any valid numeric expression.

Return Value

The same data subtype as passed to the function containing only the integer portion of *number*.

Description

Removes the fractional part of a number. Operates in a similar way to the Int function, except that if *number* is negative, Fix returns the first negative number greater than or equal to *number*. For example, Fix(-10.2) returns –10.

Int Function

Int(*number*)

number
> Type: Required, Any valid numeric datatype
>
> The number to be truncated.

Return Value

Returns a value of the numeric data subtype passed to it.

Description

Returns the integer portion of a number. Operates in a similar way to the Fix function, except that if *number* is negative, Int returns the first negative number less than or equal to *number*. For example, Int(-10.2) returns –11.

Log Function

Log(*number*)

number
> Type: Required, Double
>
> A numeric expression greater than zero.

Return Value

A Variant of subtype Double.

Description

Returns the natural logarithm of a given number.

Randomize Statement

Randomize [*number*]

number
> Type: Optional, Numeric
>
> Any valid numeric expression

Description

Initializes the random-number generator.

Rnd Function

Rnd[(*seed*)]

seed
> Type: Optional, Single
>
> Any valid numeric expression.

Return Value

A Variant of subtype Single ranging from 0 to 1.

Description

Returns a random number based on the value of *seed* as follows:

Seed	Result
< 0	The same number each time
> 0, none	The next random number in sequence
0	The most recently generated number

Round Function

Round(*expression*[, *numdecimalplaces*])

expression
> Type: Required, Numeric
>
> Any numeric expression.

numdecimalplaces
> Type: Optional, Long
>
> The number of places to include after the decimal point.

Return Value

The same data subtype as *expression*.

Description

Rounds a given number to a specified number of decimal places.

Sgn Function

Sgn(*number*)

number
> Type: Required, Any expression capable of conversion into a numeric value
>
> A numeric expression.

Return Value

A Variant of subtype Integer.

Description

Determines the sign of a number. Returns –1 for a negative expression, 1 for a positive expression, and 0 for an expression whose value is 0.

Sin Function

Sin(*number*)

number
> Type: Required, Numeric
>
> An angle expressed in radians.

Return Value

A Variant of subtype Double.

Description

Returns the sine of an angle (the ratio of two sides of a right triangle, in the range −1 to 1).

Sqr Function

Sqr(*number*)

number
> Type: Required, Double
>
> Any numeric expression greater than or equal to 0.

Return Value

A Variant of subtype Double.

Description

Calculates the square root of a given number.

Tan Function

Tan(*number*)

number
> Type: Required, Numeric expression
>
> An angle in radians.

Return Value

A Variant of subtype Double.

Description

Returns the tangent of an angle (the ratio of two sides of a right-angle triangle).

Miscellaneous

Eval Function

[*result* =]Eval(*expression*)

result
    Type: Optional, Any

    A variable to hold the result of the Eval function.

expression
    Type: Required, String Expression

    The expression to be evaluated.

Return Value

Any

Description

Evaluates an expression that can be built dynamically and returns the results.

Execute Statement

Execute *statement*

statement
    Type: Required, String expression

    A string expression containing one or more statements for execution.

Description

Executes one or more statements that can be built dynamically. The Execute statement inherits the context of the procedure that invoked it.

ExecuteGlobal Statement

ExecuteGlobal *statement*

statement
    Type: Required, String expression

    A string expression containing one or more statements for execution.

Description

Executes one or more statements that can be built dynamically. Unlike statements executed using the Execute statement, ExecuteGlobal statements execute in the script's global namespace, so that the results of executing the code (which might, for example, define a new class using the Class...End Class construct) are available to all procedures within the script.

LoadPicture Function

LoadPicture(*picturename*)

picturename
> Type: Required, String
>
> The path and filename of the picture file.

Return Value

A StdPicture object.

Description

Loads a picture object.

Object Programming

Class Statement

```
Class name
   'statements
End Class
```

name
> Type: Required, N/A
>
> The name of the class.

Description

Defines a class and delimits the statements that define that class's member variables, properties, and methods.

CreateObject Function

CreateObject(*servername.Typename* [, *Location*])

servername
> Type: Required, String
>
> The name of the application providing the object.

Typename
> Type: Required, String

> The type or class of the object to create.

Location
> Type: Optional, String

> The name of the server where the object is to be created.

Return Value

A reference to an ActiveX object.

Description

Creates an instance of an OLE Automation (ActiveX) object. Prior to calling the methods, functions, or properties of an object, you are required to create an instance of that object. Once an object is created, you reference it in code using the object variable you defined.

Note that each scripting environment also has its own object-creation facilities (e.g., `Server.CreateObject` in ASP, `WScript.CreateObject` in WSH).

For Each . . . Next Statement

```
For Each element In group
[statements]
[Exit For]
[statements]
Next [element]
```

element
> Type: Required, Variant

> A Variant to which the current element from the group is assigned.

group
> Type: Required

> A collection or an array.

statements
> Type: Optional

> A line or lines of program code to execute within the loop.

Description

Loops through the items of a collection or the elements of an array.

Function Statement

```
[Public [Default] | Private Function name
[(arglist)] [()]
    [statements]
    [name = expression]
    [Exit Function]
    [statements]
    [name = expression]
End Function
```

Public

Type: Optional, Keyword

Gives the function scope through all procedures in all modules in the project. If used within a **Class...End Class** construct, the function is also accessible from outside the project. **Public** and **Private** are mutually exclusive.

Default

Type: Optional, Keyword

Defines a method as the default member of a class. It is valid only for a public function (i.e., one defined using the **Public** keyword) defined within a **Class...End Class** statement. Only one property or method in a class block can be defined as the default member of the class.

Private

Type: Optional, Keyword

Restricts the scope of the function to those procedures within the same module.

name

Type: Required

The name of the function.

arglist

Type: Optional

A comma-delimited list of variables to be passed to the function as arguments from the calling procedure.

statements

Type: Optional

Program code to be executed within the function.

expression

Type: Optional

The value to return from the function to the calling procedure.

---

arglist uses the following syntax and parts:

```
[ByVal | ByRef] varname[( )
```

ByVal

    Type: Optional, Keyword

    The argument is passed by value; that is, the local copy of the variable is assigned the value of the argument.

ByRef

    Type: Optional, Keyword

    The argument is passed by reference; that is, the local variable is simply a reference to the argument being passed. All changes made to the local variable are also reflected in the calling argument. ByRef is the default method of passing variables.

varname

    Type: Required

    This is the name of the local variable containing either the reference or value of the argument.

Description

Defines a function procedure.

GetObject Function

```
GetObject([pathname] [, class])
```

pathname

    Type: Optional, String

    The full path and name of the file containing the ActiveX object.

class

    Type: Optional, String

    The class of the object (see the following list).

The *class* argument has these parts:

Appname

    Type: Required, String

    The name of the application.

Objecttype

    Type: Required, String

    The class of object to create, delimited from *Appname* by using a period (.). For example, Appname.Objecttype.

Return Value

Returns a reference to an ActiveX object.

Description

Accesses an ActiveX server held within a specified file and assigns its reference to an object variable.

GetRef Function

Set *object.eventname* = GetRef(*procname*)

object
Type: Required, String literal

Name of the object with which *eventname* is associated.

eventname
Type: Required, String literal

Name of the event to which the function is to be bound.

procname
Type: Required, String literal

String containing the name of the Sub or Function procedure being associated with the event.

Return Value

The address of the procedure to execute when *object.eventname* is fired.

Description

Binds a particular procedure to a DHTML event. It specifies a particular procedure as the event handler that will be executed automatically whenever the DHTML event is fired. For client-side scripting with IE only.

Initialize Event

Private Sub *object*_Initialize( )

Description

Located within a class defined by the Class...End Class construct and fired when an instance of the class is created. The event is typically used to initialize class data.

Is Operator

object1 Is *object2* | Nothing

object1
    Type: Required, Object

    An object variable.

object2
    Type: Required, Object

    A second object variable.

Return Value

Boolean.

Description

Compares two object variables to determine whether they reference the same object. The Nothing keyword can also be used to determine whether a variable contains a valid object reference.

Property Get Statement

```
[Public [Default] | Private Property Get name
[(arglist)]
    [statements]
    [name = expression]
    [Exit Property]
    [statements]
    [name = expression]
End Property
```

Public
    Type: Optional, Keyword

    Makes the property accessible from outside the class, giving it scope through all procedures in all scripts. Public and Private are mutually exclusive.

Default
    Type: Optional, Keyword

    Used only with the Public keyword to indicate that a public property is the default property of the class.

Private
    Type: Optional, Keyword

Restricts the scope of the property to those procedures within the same Class...End Class code block. Public and Private are mutually exclusive.

name
Type: Required

The name of the property.

arglist
Type: Optional, Any

A comma-delimited list of variables to be passed to the property as arguments from the calling procedure.

statements
Type: Optional

Program code to be executed within the property.

expression
Type: Optional, Any

The value to return from the property to the calling procedure.

arglist has the following syntax:

[ByVal | ByRef] *argname*[( )]

ByVal
Type: Optional

The argument is passed by value; that is, a local copy of the variable is assigned the value of the argument.

ByRef
Type: Optional

The argument is passed by reference; that is, the local variable is simply a reference to the argument being passed. Changes made to the local variable are reflected in the argument. ByRef is the default way of passing variables.

argname
Type: Required

This is the name of the local variable containing the reference of the argument.

Description

Declares the name, arguments, and code for a procedure that reads the value of a property and returns it to the calling procedure. The Property Get statement is used within a class defined by the Class...End Class construct.

Property Let Statement

```
[Public | Private Property Let name ([arglist,] value)
    [statements]
    [Exit Property]
    [statements]
End Property
```

Public

Type: Optional, Keyword

Makes the property visible outside of the class, giving it scope through all procedures in all scripts. Public and Private are mutually exclusive.

Private

Type: Optional, Keyword

Restricts the scope of the property to those procedures within the same Class...End Class code block. Private and Public are mutually exclusive.

name

Type: Required

The name of the property.

arglist

Type: Optional, Any

A comma-delimited list of variables to be passed to the property as arguments from the calling procedure.

value

Type: Required, Any

The last (or only) argument in arglist; a variable containing the value to be assigned to the property.

statements

Type: Optional

Program code to be executed within the property.

arglist uses the following syntax:

```
[ByVal | ByRef] varname[( )]
```

ByVal

Type: Optional, Keyword

The argument is passed by value; that is, a local copy of the variable is assigned the value of the argument.

ByRef
Type: Optional, Keyword

The argument is passed by reference; that is, the local variable is simply a reference to the argument being passed. All changes made to the local variable are reflected in the calling argument when control returns to the calling procedure. ByRef is the default method of passing variables.

varname
Type: Required

This is the name of the local variable containing either the reference or value of the argument.

Description

Declares the name, arguments, and code for a procedure that assigns a value to a property. The Property Let statement is used within a class defined by the Class...End Class construct.

Property Set Statement

```
[Public | Private Property Set name
   ([arglist,] reference)
   [statements]
   [Exit Property]
   [statements]
End Property
```

Public
Type: Optional, Keyword

Makes the property accessible from outside the class, so that it is visible to all procedures in all scripts. Public and Private are mutually exclusive.

Private
Type: Optional, Keyword

Restricts the scope of the property to code within the Class...End Class construct in which the property is declared. Public and Private are mutually exclusive.

name
Type: Required

The name of the property.

arglist
  Type: Optional, Any

  A comma-delimited list of variables to be passed to the property as arguments from the calling procedure.

reference
  Type: Required, Object

  The last (or only) argument in *arglist*; it must be a variable containing the object reference to be assigned to the property.

statements
  Type: Optional

  Program code to be executed within the property.

arglist uses the following syntax and parts:

  [ByVal | ByRef] *varname*[( )]

  ByVal
    Type: Optional, Keyword

    The argument is passed by value; that is, a local copy of the variable is assigned the value of the argument.

  ByRef
    Type: Optional, Keyword

    The argument is passed by reference; that is, the local variable is simply a reference to the argument being passed. All changes made to the local variable are reflected in the calling argument when control returns to the calling procedure. ByRef is the default method of passing variables.

  varname
    Type: Required, Any

    This is the name of the local variable containing either the reference or value of the argument.

Description

Declares the name, arguments, and code for a procedure that assigns an object reference to a property. The **Property Set** statement is used within a class defined by the **Class...End Class** construct.

Property Set contrasts with **Property Let**, which assigns a value that is not an object reference to a property.

Set Statement

Syntax 1

```
Set objectvar = {[objectexpression | new classname |
Nothing}
```

objectvar
   Type: Required, Object

   The name of the object variable or property.

objectexpression
   Type: Optional, Object

   An expression evaluating to an object.

new
   Type: Optional, Keyword

   Creates a new instance of an object defined using the
   Class...End Class construct.

classname
   Type: Required, String literal

   The name of the class defined by the Class...End Class construct to be instantiated.

Nothing
   Type: Optional, Keyword

   Assigns the special datatype Nothing to *objectvar*, thereby
   releasing the reference to the object.

Syntax 2

```
Set object.eventname = GetRef(procname)
```

object.eventname
   Type: Required, Event

   The name of an object event that, when fired, causes the code
   in *procname* to execute.

procname
   Type: Required, String literal

   The name of the procedure that serves as the event handler for
   object.eventname.

Description

Assigns an object reference to a variable or property. Its second
syntax, using the GetRef function, defines an event handler for an
event; this is discussed in the GetRef function entry.

Sub Statement

```
[Public [Default] | Private] Sub name
    [(arglist)]
    [statements]
    [Exit Sub]
    [statements]
End Sub
```

Public

> Type: Optional, Keyword

> Gives the subprocedure scope through all procedures in all modules in the project. If used within a creatable class module, the subprocedure is also accessible from outside the project. Public and Private are mutually exclusive.

Default

> Type: Optional, Keyword

> Indicates that a public procedure defined in a VBScript class (that is, defined within a Class...End Class construct) is the default member of the class.

Private

> Type: Optional, Keyword

> Restricts the scope of the subprocedure to those procedures within the same module. Public, Private, and Friend are mutually exclusive.

name

> Type: Required

> The name of the subprocedure.

arglist

> Type: Optional, Any

> A comma-delimited list of variables to be passed to the subprocedure as arguments from the calling procedure.

statements

> Type: Optional

> Program code to be executed within the subprocedure.

arglist uses the following syntax and parts:

> [ByVal | ByRef] *varname*[( )]

> ByVal

>> Type: Optional

>> The argument is passed by value; that is, a local copy of the variable is assigned the value of the argument.

ByRef
Type: Optional

The argument is passed by reference; that is, the local variable is simply a reference to the argument being passed. All changes made to the local variable are also reflected in the calling argument. ByRef is the default method of passing variables.

varname
Type: Required

This is the name of the local variable containing the reference or argument value.

Description

Defines a subprocedure.

Terminate Event

Private Sub Class_Terminate( )

Description

Fired when the last instance of an object or class is removed from memory.

With Statement

With *object*
    [*statements*]
End With

object
Type: Required, Object

A previously declared object variable.

statements
Type: Optional

Program code to execute against object.

Description

Performs a set of property assignments and executes other code against a particular object, thus allowing you to refer to the object only once. Because the object is referred to only once, the "behind the scenes" qualification of that object is also performed only once, leading to improved performance of the code block.

Program Structure and Flow

Call Statement

[Call] *procedurename* ([*argumentlist*])

Call
> Type: Optional

procedurename
> Type: Required, N/A

> The name of the subroutine being called.

argumentlist
> Type: Optional, Any

> A comma-delimited list of arguments to pass to the subroutine being called.

Description

Passes program control to an explicitly named procedure or function. If you do not include the Call keyword, the argument list should not be enclosed in parentheses.

Do . . . Loop Statement

```
Do [{While | Until} condition]
    [statements]
[Exit Do]
    [statements]
Loop
```

or:

```
Do
    [statements]
[Exit Do]
    [statements]
Loop [{While | Until} condition]
```

condition
> Type: Optional, Boolean expression

> An expression that evaluates to True or False.

statements
> Type: Optional

> Program statements that are repeatedly executed while or until *condition* is True.

Description

Repeatedly executes a block of code while or until a condition becomes True.

End . . . Statement

```
End Class
End Function
End If
End Property
End Select
End Sub
End Type
End With
```

Description

Ends a procedure or a block of code.

Exit Statement

```
Exit Do
Exit For
Exit Function
Exit Property
Exit Sub
```

Description

Prematurely exits a block of code.

For Each . . . Next Statement

See "For Each . . . Next Statement" entry under "Object-Oriented Programming."

For . . . Next Statement

```
For counter = initial_value To maximum_value
                        Step stepcounter]
    ' ... code to execute on each iteration ...
   [Exit For]
Next [counter]
```

counter

> Type: Required (optional with Next statement), Numeric.
>
> Any valid numeric variable to be used as the loop counter.

---

initial_value
> Type: Required, Numeric
>
> Any valid numeric expression that specifies the loop counter's initial value.

maximum_value
> Type: Required, Numeric
>
> Any valid numeric expression that specifies the loop counter's maximum value.

stepcounter
> Type: Optional (required if Step used), Numeric
>
> Any valid numeric expression that indicates how much the loop counter should be incremented with each new iteration of the loop.

Description

Defines a loop that executes a given number of times, as determined by a loop counter. To use the For...Next loop, you must assign a numeric value to a counter variable. This counter is either incremented or decremented automatically with each iteration of the loop. In the For statement, you specify the value that is to be assigned to the counter initially and the maximum value the counter will reach for the block of code to be executed. The Next statement marks the end of the block of code that is to execute repeatedly.

Function Statement

See "Function Statement" entry under "Object Programming."

If . . . Then . . . Else Statement

```
If condition Then
    [statements]
[ElseIf condition-n Then
    [elseifstatements] ...
[Else
    [elsestatements]]
End If
```

Or, you can use the single-line syntax:

```
If cond Then [statements] [Else elsestatements]
```

---

condition (cond)
  Type: Required, Boolean

  An expression returning either True or False or an object type.

statements
  Type: Optional

  Program code to be executed if *condition* is True.

condition-n
  Type: Optional

  Same as *condition*.

elseifstatements
  Type: Optional

  Program code to be executed if the corresponding *condition-n*
  is True.

elsestatements
  Type: Optional

  Program code to be executed if the corresponding *condition* or
  condition-n is False.

Description

Executes a statement or block of statements based on the Boolean
(True or False) value of an expression.

Private Statement

```
Private varname[([subscripts])]
          [, varname[([subscripts])]] ...
```

varname
  Type: Required, Any

  The name of the variable.

subscripts
  Type: Optional, Integer or Long

  Denotes *varname* as an array and optionally specifies the number and extent of array dimensions.

Description

Used in a script or class to declare a private or local variable and
allocate the relevant storage space in memory.

Property Get Statement

See "Property Get Statement" entry under "Object Programming."

Property Let Statement

See "Property Let Statement" entry under "Object Programming."

Property Set Statement

See "Property Set Statement" entry under "Object Programming."

Public Statement

```
Public varname[([subscripts])] _
    varname[([subscripts])]
```

varname
    Type: Required, Any

    The name of the variable.

subscripts
    Type: Optional, Integer or Long

    Denotes *varname* as an array and optionally specifies the dimensions and number of elements of the array.

Description

Used in a script or a Class block to declare a public variable. A Public variable has script-level scope—that is, it can be used by all procedures in a script. When used in a class construct, it is visible outside the class project.

Select Case Statement

```
Select Case testexpression
    [Case expressionlist
        [statements-n]] ...
    [Case Else
        [elsestatements]]
End Select
```

testexpression
    Type: Required, Any

    Any numeric or string expression whose value determines which block of code is executed.

expressionlist
   Type: Required, Any

   Comma-delimited list of expressions to compare values with *testexpression*.

statements-n
   Type: Optional

   Program statements to execute if a match is found between any section of *expressionlist* and *testexpression*.

elsestatements
   Type: Optional

   Program statements to execute if a match between *testexpression* and any *expressionlist* can't be found.

Description

Allows for the conditional execution of a block of code, typically out of three or more code blocks, based on some condition. Use the Select Case statement as an alternative to complex nested If...Then...Else statements.

Sub Statement

See "Sub Statement" entry under "Object Programming."

While ... Wend Statement

```
While condition
   [statements]
Wend
```

condition
   Type: Required, Boolean

   An expression evaluating to True or False.

statements
   Type: Optional

   Program statements to execute while condition remains True.

Description

Repeatedly executes program code while a given condition remains True.

With Statement

See "With Statement" entry under "Object Programming."

String Manipulation

Asc, AscB, AscW Functions

See "Asc, AscB, AscW Functions" entry under "Data Subtype Conversion."

Chr, ChrB, ChrW Functions

See "Chr, ChrB, ChrW Functions" entry under "Data Subtype Conversion."

Filter Function

See "Filter Function" entry under "Array Handling."

FormatCurrency, FormatNumber, FormatPercent Functions

```
FormatCurrency(number[,DecimalPlaces ][, _
IncLeadingZero[,UseParenthesis[,GroupDigits]]]])
```

```
FormatNumber(number[,DecimalPlaces ][, _
IncLeadingZero[,UseParenthesis[,GroupDigits]]]])
```

```
FormatPercent(number[,DecimalPlaces ][, _
IncLeadingZero[,UseParenthesis[,GroupDigits]]]])
```

number
> Type: Required, Any numeric expression
>
> The number to be formatted.

DecimalPlaces
> Type: Optional, Long
>
> Number of digits the formatted string should contain after the decimal point.

IncLeadingZero
> Type: Optional, Long
>
> Indicates if the formatted string is to have a 0 before floating-point numbers between 1 and –1.

UseParenthesis
> Type: Optional, Long
>
> Specifies whether parentheses should be placed around negative numbers.

GroupDigits

Type: Optional, Long

Determines whether digits in the returned string should be grouped using the delimiter specified in the computer's regional settings. For example, on English language systems, the value 1000000 is returned as 1,000,000 if *GroupDigits* is True.

Return Value

String

Description

The three functions are almost identical. They all take identical arguments, the only difference being that FormatCurrency returns a formatted number beginning with the currency symbol specified in the computer's regional settings, FormatNumber returns just the formatted number, and FormatPercent returns the formatted number followed by a percentage sign (%).

FormatDateTime Function

FormatDateTime(*date*[,*format*])

date

Type: Required, Date or String

Any expression that can be evaluated as a date.

format

Type: Optional, Long

Defines the format. Possible values are vbGeneralDate (the default), vbLongDate, vbShortDate, vbLongTime, and vbShortTime.

Return Value

String

Description

Formats a date or time expression based on the computer's regional settings.

InStr, InStrB Functions

InStr([*start*,]*stringtosearch*, *stringtofind*
    [, *compare*])

start
> Type: Optional, Numeric

> The starting position for the search.

stringtosearch
> Type: Required, String

> The string being searched.

stringtofind
> Type: Required, String

> The string being sought.

compare
> Type: Optional, Integer

> The method that compares *stringtofind* with *stringtosearch*; its value can be vbBinaryCompare or vbTextCompare.

Return Value

A Variant of subtype Long.

Description

Finds the starting position of one string within another.

InstrRev Function

```
InstrRev(sourcestring, soughtstring[, start
      [, compare]])
```

sourcestring
> Type: Required, String

> The string to be searched.

soughtstring
> Type: Required, String

> The substring to be found within *sourcestring*.

start
> Type: Optional, Numeric

> Starting position of the search. If no value is specified, *start* defaults to 1.

compare
> Type: Optional, Integer

> The method that compares *soughtstring* with *sourcestring*; its value can be vbBinaryCompare or vbTextCompare.

Return Value

Variant of subtype Long.

Description

Determines the starting position of a substring within a string by searching from the end of the string to its beginning.

Join Function

See "Join Function" entry under "Array Handling."

LCase Function

LCase(*string*)

string
 Type: Required, String
 A valid string expression.

Return Value

A Variant of subtype String.

Description

Converts each character in a string to lowercase.

Left, LeftB Functions

Left(*string, length*)

string
 Type: Required, String
 The string to be processed.
length
 Type: Required, Long
 The number of characters to return from the left of the string.

Return Value

Left and LeftB return a Variant of subtype String.

Description

Returns a string containing the leftmost *length* characters of *string*.

Len, LenB Functions

See "Filter Function" entry under "Information Functions."

LTrim Function

LTrim(*stringexp*)

stringexp
  Type: Required, String
  A valid string expression.

Return Value

A Variant of subtype String.

Description

Removes any leading spaces from *stringexp*.

Match Object

Description

A member of the Matches collection that is returned by a call to the RegExp object's Execute method, the Match object represents a successful regular-expression match.

Creatable

No

Returned by

Matches.Item property.

Properties

The Match object supports the following three properties:

FirstIndex (Long)
  Indicates the position in the original search string where the regular-expression match occurred. The first character in the search string is at position 1.

Length (Long)
  Indicates the number of characters in the match found in the search string. This is also the number of characters in the Match object's Value property.

Value (String)
  The text of the match found in the search string.

Matches Collection Object

Description

The collection of zero or more Match objects returned by the RegExp object's Execute method; each Match object allows you to identify and manipulate one of the strings found by the regular expression.

Creatable

No

Returned by

RegExp.Execute method

Properties

The Matches collection object supports the following two read-only properties:

Count (Long)
> Indicates the number of objects in the collection. A value of zero indicates that the collection is empty.

Item (Match object)
> Syntax: Matches.Item(*index*)
>
> Returns a particular Match object based on *index*, its ordinal position in the collection. Matches is a zero-based collection; that is, its first member is at ordinal position 0, while its last member is at ordinal position Matches.Count   1.

Mid, MidB Functions

Mid(*string*, start[, *length*])

string
> Type: Required, String
>
> The expression from which to return a substring.

start
> Type: Required, Long
>
> The starting position of the substring.

length
> Type: Optional, Long
>
> The length of the substring.

Return Value

A Variant of subtype String.

Description

Returns a substring of a specified length from within a given string.

RegExp Object

Description

The RegExp object provides support for regular-expression matching—for the ability to search strings for substrings matching general or specific patterns.

In order to conduct a pattern search, you must first instantiate the regular-expression object, with code like the following:

```
Dim oRegExp        ' Instance of RegExp object
Set oRegExp = New RegExp
```

To conduct a search using the RegExp object, do the following:

- Set the IgnoreCase property to determine whether the search should be case-sensitive.
- Set the Global property to determine whether all instances or just the first instance of the substring should be returned.
- Assign the Pattern string that you want to find to the Pattern property.
- Provide a string that the RegExp object is to search when calling one of the RegExp object's methods.

The RegExp.Execute Method allows you to search for a substring that matches your pattern string in any of three ways:

- You can determine whether a pattern match is found in the string.
- You can return one or all of the occurrences of the matching substrings. In this case, results are returned in Match objects within the Matches collection.
- You can replace all substrings matching the pattern string with another string.

Properties

The RegExp object supports the following three properties:

Global (Boolean)
 Indicates whether to search for all occurrences of the pattern string or just for the first one. Its default value is False; a search will stop once the first match is found.

IgnoreCase (Boolean)
 Indicates whether the pattern search is case-sensitive. Its default value is False; searches will be case-sensitive.

Pattern (String)

    Indicates the pattern string to search for. The pattern string can consist of character literals along with the special characters shown in the "Regular Expression Characters Reference" section.

Methods

The RegExp object supports the following three methods:

Execute

    Returns a Matches collection containing information about the substrings in a larger string that match a pattern string. Its syntax is:

```
oRegExp.Execute(string)
```

    where *string* is the string to be searched.

Replace

    Replaces all substrings in a larger string, which match a pattern string, with a second string. Its syntax is:

```
oRegExp.Replace(string1, string2)
```

    where *string1* is the string to be searched and *string2* is the string that's to replace substring matches within *string1*.

Test

    Returns a Boolean that indicates whether the search of a string has succeeded in finding a pattern match. Its syntax is:

```
oRegExp.Test string
```

    where *string* is the string to be searched.

Replace Function

```
Replace(string, stringToReplace, replacementString
      [, start[, count[, compare]]])
```

string

    Type: Required, String

    The complete string containing the substring to be replaced.

stringToReplace

    Type: Required, String

    The substring to be found by the function.

replacementString

    Type: Required, String

    The new substring to replace *stringToReplace* in *string*.

---

start

> Type: Optional, Long

> The character position in *string* at which the search for *stringToReplace* begins.

count

> Type: Optional, Long

> The number of instances of *stringToReplace* to replace.

compare

> Type: Optional, Integer

> The method that compares *stringToReplace* with *string*; its value can be vbBinaryCompare or vbTextCompare.

Return Value

The return value from Replace depends on the parameters you specify in the argument list, as the following table shows:

If	Return Value
string = ""	Zero-length string ("")
string is Null	An error
StringToReplace = ""	Copy of *string*
replacementString = ""	Copy of *string* with all instances of *stringToReplace* removed
start > Len(string)	Zero-length string ("")
count = 0	Copy of *string*

Description

Replaces a given number of instances of a specified substring in another string.

Right, RightB Functions

Right(*string*, *length*)

string

> Type: Required, String

> The string to be processed.

length

> Type: Required, Long

> The number of characters to return from the right of the string.

Return Value

A Variant of subtype String.

Description

Returns a string containing the rightmost *length* characters of *string*.

RTrim Function

RTrim(*stringexp*)

stringexp
    Type: Required, String
    A valid string expression.

Return Value

A Variant of subtype String.

Description

Removes any trailing spaces from *stringexp*.

Space Function

Space(*number*)

number
    Type: Required, Integer
    An expression evaluating to the number of spaces required.

Return Value

A Variant of subtype String.

Description

Creates a string containing *number* spaces.

Split Function

See the "Split Function" entry under "Array Handling."

StrComp Function

StrComp(*string1*, *string2*[, *compare*])

string1
> Type: Required, String

> Any string expression.

string2
> Type: Required, String

> Any string expression.

compare
> Type: Optional, Integer constant

> The type of string comparison to perform. Possible values are vbBinaryCompare and vbTextCompare.

Return Value

A Variant of subtype Integer.

Description

Determines whether two strings are equal and which of two strings is greater, as shown in the following table:

If	Returns
string1 < string2	−1
string1 = string2	0
string1 > string2	1
string1 or string2 is Null	Null

String Function

String(*number, character*)

number
> Type: Required, Long

> The length of the required string.

character
> Type: Required, Variant

> Character or character code used to create the required string.

Return Value

A Variant of subtype String.

Description

Creates a string comprising a single character repeated a specified number of times.

StrReverse Function

StrReverse(*str_expression*)

str_expression
> Type: Required, String

> The string whose characters are to be reversed.

Return Value

A Variant of subtype String.

Description

Returns a string that is the reverse of the string passed to it. For example, if the string and is passed to it as an argument, StrReverse returns the string dna.

Trim Function

Trim(*string*)

string
> Type: Required, String

> Any string expression.

Return Value

A Variant of subtype String.

Description

Removes both leading and trailing spaces from a given string.

UCase Function

UCase(*string*)

string
> Type: Required, String

> A valid string expression.

Return Value

A Variant of subtype String.

Description

Converts each character in a string to uppercase.

User Interaction

InputBox Function

```
InputBox(prompt[, title] [, default] [, xpos]
            [, ypos] [, helpfile, context])
```

prompt
    Type: Required, String

    The message in the dialog box.

title
    Type: Optional, String

    The titlebar of the dialog box.

default
    Type: Optional, String

    String to be displayed in the text box on loading.

xpos
    Type: Optional, Numeric

    The distance from the left side of the screen to the left side of the dialog box.

ypos
    Type: Optional, Numeric

    The distance from the top of the screen to the top of the dialog box.

helpfile
    Type: Optional, String

    The Help file to use if the user clicks the Help button on the dialog box.

context
    Type: Optional, Numeric

    The context number to use within the Help file specified in *helpfile*.

Return Value

InputBox returns a Variant string containing the contents of the text box from the InputBox dialog.

Description

Displays a dialog box containing a label, which prompts the user about the data you expect him to input, a text box for entering the data, an OK button, a Cancel button, and optionally a Help button.

When the user clicks OK, the function returns the contents of the
text box. The InputBox function cannot be used in an ASP script
running on the server.

MsgBox Function

```
MsgBox(prompt[, buttons][, title]
          [, helpfile, context])
```

prompt
    Type: Required, String

    The text of the message to display in the message box.

buttons
    Type: Optional, Numeric

    The sum of the Button, Icon, Default Button, and Modality con-
    stant values.

title
    Type: Optional, String

    The title displayed in the titlebar of the message box.

helpfile
    Type: Optional, String

    An expression specifying the name of the Help file to provide
    help functionality for the dialog.

context
    Type: Optional, Numeric

    An expression specifying a context ID within *helpfile*.

Return Value

A Variant of subtype Integer indicating the button clicked by the
user.

Description

Displays a dialog box containing a message, buttons, and optional
icon to the user. The action taken by the user is returned by the
function as an integer value. MsgBox cannot be used in an ASP
script running on the server.

Variable Declaration

Const Statement

See "Const Statement" entry under "Constants."

Dim Statement

See "Dim Statement" entry under "Array Handling."

Option Explicit Statement

```
Option Explicit
```

Description

Generates a compile-time error whenever a variable that has not been declared is encountered. `Option Explicit` must precede any VBScript source code, or an error results.

Private Statement

See "Private Statement" entry under "Program Structure and Flow."

Public Statement

See "Public Statement" entry under "Program Structure and Flow."

ReDim Statement

See "ReDim Statement" entry under "Array Handling."

Regular Expression Characters Reference

Symbol	Description
\	Marks the next character either as a special character (such as \n for the newline character) or as a literal (if that character otherwise has special meaning in a pattern search string). The special characters are: \f Form feed character \n Newline character \r Carriage return character \t Tab character \v Vertical tab character
^	Matches the beginning of input.
$	Matches the end of input.

Symbol	Description
*	Matches the preceding character zero or more times.
+	Matches the preceding character one or more times.
?	Matches the preceding character zero or one time.
.	Matches any single character except a newline character.
( )	Defines a subexpression within the larger subexpression. A subexpression: • Overrides the order of precedence used in evaluating pattern strings. • Can be referenced again in the pattern string. To insert the *result* of the subexpression later in the pattern string, reference it by its one-based ordinal position among subexpressions, preceded by the backslash symbol (e.g., \1). • Can be referenced again in the replacement string in calls to the RegExp.Replace method. To use the *result* of the original subexpression as a replacement string, reference its one-based ordinal position among subexpressions, preceded by a dollar sign (e.g., $1).
x|y	Matches either x or y.
{*n*}	Matches exactly *n* times, where *n* is a non-negative integer.
{*n*,}	Matches at least *n* times, where *n* is a non-negative integer. o{1,} is the same as o+, and o{0,} is the same as o*.
{*n*,*m*}	Matches at least *n* and at most *m* times, where *m* and *n* are non-negative integers. o{0,1} is the same as o?.
[*abc*]	Matches any one of the enclosed characters (represented by *abc*) in the character set.
[^*xyz*]	Matches any character (represented by *xyz*) not enclosed in the character set. For example, [^abc] matches the p in plain.
[*a-z*]	Matches any character in a range of characters (represented by *a-z*).
[^*m-z*]	Matches any character not included in a range of characters (represented by *m-z*).
\b	Matches a word boundary, that is, the position between a word and a space. The word-boundary symbol does not include newline characters or the end of input (see the \s symbol).

Symbol	Description
\B	Matches a nonword boundary. ea*r\B matches the ear in never early.
\d	Matches a digit character. Equivalent to [0-9].
\D	Matches a nondigit character. Equivalent to [^0-9].
\s	Matches any whitespace, including space, tab, form-feed, and so on. Equivalent to [\f\n\r\t\v].
\S	Matches any nonwhitespace character. Equivalent to [^ \f\n\r\t\v].
\w	Matches any word character including underscore. Equivalent to [A-Za-z0-9_].
\W	Matches any nonword character, including whitespace and carriage returns. Equivalent to [^A-Za-z0-9_].
\num	Matches the subexpression (enclosed in parentheses) whose ordinal position in the pattern is num, where num is a positive integer.
\n	Matches n, where n is the octal value of an ASCII code. Octal escape values must be 1, 2, or 3 digits long and must not exceed 256; if they do, only the first 2 digits are used.
\xn	Matches n, where n is the hexadecimal value of an ASCII code. Hexadecimal escape values must be two digits long.

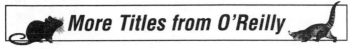

More Titles from O'Reilly

Visual Basic Programming

Visual Basic Shell Programming

By J. P. Hamilton
1st Edition July 2000
392 pages, ISBN 1-56592-670-6

VB & VBA in a Nutshell: The Language

By Paul Lomax
1st Edition October 1998
656 pages, ISBN 1-56592-358-8

Access Database Design & Programming, 2nd Edition

By Steven Roman
2nd Edition July 1999
432 pages, ISBN 1-56592-626-9

Visual Basic Controls in a Nutshell

By Evan S. Dictor
1st Edition July 1999
762 pages, ISBN 1-56592-294-8

VBScript in a Nutshell

By Paul Lomax, Matt Childs, & Ron Petrusha
1st Edition May 2000
512 pages, ISBN 1-56592-720-6

ASP In a Nutshell, 2nd Edition

By A. Keyton Weissinger
2nd Edition July 2000
492 pages, ISBN 1-56592-843-1

Developing ASP Components, 2nd Edition

By Shelley Powers
2nd Edition January 2001 (est.)
600 pages (est.), ISBN 1-56592-750-8

ADO: The Definitive Guide

By Jason T. Roff
1st Edition February 2001 (est.)
450 pages (est.), ISBN 1-56592-415-0

Writing Excel Macros

By Steven Roman
1st Edition May 1999
552 pages, ISBN 1-56592-587-4

Win32 API Programming with Visual Basic

By Steve Roman
1st Edition November 1999
534 pages, Includes CD-ROM
ISBN 1-56592-631-5

Windows Users